DECEIVED BY GOD?

DECEIVED BY GOD?

A Journey Through Suffering

JOHN S. FEINBERG

CROSSWAY BOOKS • WHEATON, ILLINOIS
A DIVISION OF GOOD NEWS PUBLISHERS

Deceived by God?

Copyright © 1997 by John S. Feinberg

Published by Crossway Books
a division of Good News Publishers
1300 Crescent Street
Wheaton, Illinois 60187

Cover Design: D² DesignWorks

Cover Photograph: Tony Stone Images / Chris Windsor

First printing, 1997

Printed in the United States of America

Library of Congress Cataloging-in-Publication Data
Feinberg, John S., 1946-
    Deceived by God? : a journey through suffering /
John S. Feinberg.
        p.   cm.
    ISBN 0-89107-886-X
    1. Suffering—Religious aspects—Christianity.   2. Good and evil.
    3. Theodicy.   4. Feinberg, John S., 1946- .   I. Title.
BT732.7.F445   1997
231'.8—dc20   96-44166

05		04		03		02		01		00		99		98		97
15	14	13	12	11	10	9	8	7	6	5	4	3	2	1

Dedicated to

Josiah Stephen
Jonathan Seth
Jeremy Samuel

three gifts of God's love

CONTENTS

PREFACE

This is a book that I never wanted to write. Even more, I wish I had not learned the things I will share in the way I did. Of course, God's plans for us are often different than we envision.

During doctoral studies in philosophy at the University of Chicago, I was given permission to write my dissertation on the problem of evil. After graduation, I had it published, but it remained in print for only a few years. Believing that it had a message that needed to be in print, I received a contract from another publisher to expand and republish the work. I originally planned to update the bibliography, and perhaps to add a chapter or two on new philosophical developments in regard to the issue. By the time I actually had enough time to make revisions, there were many developments in the intellectual discussions over the problem of evil. Clearly, more than a mere updating of bibliography was necessary.

Preface

In addition to developments in intellectual discussions about the problem of evil, the events I relate in this book began to happen. For a long time, it was very painful for me even to think about what was happening, let alone speak or write about it. But over a period of time the Lord gave me enough strength to begin talking about what was occurring in my family's life and what I was learning through it. As I saw how positively people responded, I gradually became convinced that God wanted me to put my thoughts in writing. As a result, when I completed revising my doctoral dissertation, I included two chapters on what is called "the religious problem of evil." In those chapters, I talked about the personal and religious dimensions of struggles with pain and suffering.

I thought that would be the end of it. To my surprise, my editor suggested that while those chapters were a fitting climax to my technical treatment of the problem of evil, they contained a message that would benefit philosophers and non-philosophers alike. He suggested that in addition to including them with the longer book, I should take them out of that other book and reformulate them for a more popular treatment that deals just with the religious problem of evil. The idea for this book was born.

For those who read this book and would like to delve further into more theoretical questions about why an all-powerful,

A Journey Through Suffering

all-loving God would allow evil in our world, I refer you to my lengthier book, entitled *The Many Faces of Evil* (Grand Rapids, Mich: Zondervan Publishing House, 1994). In it I distinguish between the religious problem of evil and the many intellectual problems of evil. There are chapters discussing how various Christian theistic systems would solve the problems of moral evil, natural evil, the amount of evil, the apparent purposelessness of some evils, and the like. You will also find my chapters on the personal dimensions of struggling with evil, but they appear in a different form than here. In this book, I have expanded my coverage of the religious problem. I have also included an *Afterword* by my wife, Pat, in which she offers her reflections on what has happened to her and what God has taught her through these experiences.

Perhaps you will wonder why there is no reference in this book to other works such as C.S. Lewis's classic *A Grief Observed*, or to the wonderful treatments of the practical dimensions of the problem of evil in such books as D.A. Carson's *How Long, Oh Lord?* and Nicholas Wolterstorff's *Lament for a Son*. Those books and others are well worth reading. However, I have not cited or mentioned them because I believe that what has happened to my wife and family and what God has taught me is in various ways unique. My story is also a very personal one, one that I would just as soon have kept private. Through

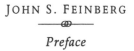
the leading of the Lord and the encouragement of others, I have seen that I should tell this story, but I wanted it to be *my* story told in *my* words. If all I were to do is repeat what others have said, there would be no need for this book. After all, it is not a research project, but a personal testimony of God's specific dealings with me and my family. So I have told the story without reference to these other works, but I would highly recommend them to anyone interested in further answers to the religious problem of evil.

To produce a book such as this requires the encouragement and help of many people. I must initially express my sincere appreciation to Stan Gundry and Jim Ruark of Zondervan, who helped produce *The Many Faces of Evil*. My deepest appreciation is also due to Leonard Goss and Lane Dennis, as well as the whole editorial staff at Crossway Books. Not only did Len and Lane believe in the project, but they have been extremely helpful in suggesting ways to make the adjustment from a more technical work to a more popular one. Friends and colleagues read earlier drafts of this work and offered helpful suggestions and encouraged me to put this in print. Special thanks are due in that regard to Paul Feinberg, Wayne Grudem, Ted Olsen, Grant Osborne, and Bruce Ware. It also goes without saying that this book would be impossible without the love and support of my wife and family. Since this story is not simply about me, but about my whole family, without their approval and encouragement I would not make this story public. Moreover, I believe that you will find Pat's *Afterword* very moving and encouraging as you confront your own trials and afflictions.

My goal is to minister to those who are suffering and struggling with their relationship to God as a result of that affliction. I hope that this book will also help those who minister to the afflicted. May God be pleased to use it in these ways!

1

PRELUDE
TO A PROBLEM

—— ⊕ ——

MANY CHRISTIANS LOVE TO SING THE HYMNS "HAVE
Thine Own Way, Lord" and "Where He leads Me I Will
Follow." These hymns express a basic longing of every Christian,
the desire to know and obey God's will. But is it possible to know
God's will for our lives?

Will God reveal his will, if we seek it? Does he ever hide
information from us to get us to do his will? Is it possible to seek
God's will, find it and do it, and then discover that what he
wanted brought great suffering and evil into your life? If that
happened, wouldn't it mean that God tricked or even deceived
you into doing his will?

Preposterous, you reply! That couldn't happen. Such questions aren't worth thinking about, for God just doesn't work that
way. Scripture tells us to seek God's will and to pray for it. In fact,
Jesus told his disciples that when they pray, they should ask God

to do his will on earth as it is done in heaven (Matt. 6:10). So, of course, God's people should ask him to do his will on earth in their own lives. The apostle John also tells us that if we pray according to God's will, he will grant our requests (1 John 5:14-15).

There you have it. We must seek God's will and pray in accordance with it. But if we find God's will and pray according to it, God wouldn't give us something evil, would he? After all, as Jesus said:

> *"Which of you, if his son asks for bread, will give him a stone? Or if he asks for a fish, will give him a snake? If you, then, though you are evil, know how to give good gifts to your children, how much more will your Father in heaven give good gifts to those who ask Him!"*
>
> —*Matthew 7:9-11*

Surely, then, if God reveals his will and we do it, evil won't befall us. God won't give us a stone when we ask for a loaf or a snake when we ask for a fish, especially not when we ask according to his will for us. Thoughts to the contrary must be absurd, if not blasphemous. They imagine the unthinkable, the impossible.

Or do they? For most of my life I would not have even

A Journey Through Suffering

thought to raise such questions. Oh, I knew bad things happen to good people. For much of my life I have wondered why God lets bad things happen to us, if he really loves us. I have pondered whether I would still want to worship and serve him if he rewarded my faithfulness with severe affliction. However, I never imagined that this affliction might come in the process of seeking, finding, and doing God's will. Nor would I have thought that God's ways might include getting someone to do his will by withholding information from him or her. That would seem like trickery, even deceit, and it would also be cruel, especially if by doing God's will we wound up in the midst of severe affliction. Who would think God does this to get his way?

And yet, several years ago something happened that led me to raise these questions and to think the unthinkable. Throughout my life I have thought a lot about the problem of evil, the question of why there is evil and suffering in our world if there is a God who loves us enough to stop it—and has power enough to do so. In fact, I even wrote my doctoral dissertation in philosophy at the University of Chicago on the problem of evil. I learned that there is a difference between asking why there is evil *in general* if an all-loving, all-powerful God exists, and asking why God allows a *specific* evil to happen to someone.

Philosophers and theologians debate on the intellectual level how the evil in our world is consistent with an all-powerful, all-loving God. On the other hand, the *personal experience* of evil creates a different kind of problem. Those confronted with personal affliction may find that their suffering disrupts their relation to God. They may find it hard to worship or serve God. They may even be tempted to stop believing in God altogether. This personal struggle with evil is a different problem than questions about God and evil in general. "Such a problem calls, not for philosophical enlightenment, but for pastoral care."[1]

I read that last statement many years ago. I had always seen the problem of evil as a major hindrance in getting non-Christians to consider Christ. I knew it could be devastating to the faith of Christians as well. But I thought that as long as one had intellectual answers to explain why God allowed evil in the world, that would satisfy those who suffered. The intellectual answers would give the necessary strength to withstand the afflictions. Even more, I thought that if comforters could just inform those who suffer of all the positive things God might do in their lives in the midst of affliction, they might come to a point where they could thank God for the affliction.

When I saw others struggle over their relationship with God because of some tragedy, I was somewhat impatient with them when they seemed unable to move past these struggles. I agreed that sufferers need pastoral care, but I thought that a lot of that care involved explaining intellectually God's purposes in allowing evil. Maybe personal struggles in the face of evil are not problems needing philosophical enlightenment, but a healthy dose of academic philosophy couldn't hurt. Or so I thought.

In recent years I have come to see things quite differently, especially because of the way that evil has deeply touched my wife and family. Before these things happened, I could not have written this book. I thought it was enough just to have intellectual answers, and that those answers would be sufficient for handling any personal evil that might come into my own life. Also, for a long time after we learned about my wife's condition, I found it too painful to speak about what had happened, let alone write about it.

What happened that so revolutionized my thinking? Let me tell you my story. Like many people, I grew up, went to school, got married, and began a career in relatively trouble-free circumstances. There were problems and afflictions along the way, like most people experience, but nothing catastrophic or truly tragic. I knew that those who stand for Christ can expect to suffer, so I figured there were more troubles coming. I assumed that they would be like the rest I had endured—annoying, frustrating, and painful to a certain degree, but nothing totally devastating. After all, I reasoned, once one goes a certain distance with Christ and reaches a certain level of spiritual maturity, even really big problems won't derail spiritual growth. There might be temporary setbacks in one's relation to the Lord, but they would soon be over.

All of that changed for me on November 4, 1987, when I learned something that went far beyond my worst nightmare. For some years my wife, Pat, had experienced certain physical difficulties. They were not painful, and neither one of us thought of them as real physical problems. They were symptoms of something, even though we had no idea of what. As the years passed, the difficulties became more pronounced. We decided that we had to find out what the problem was and get it corrected. My wife eventually went to a neurologist, who made the diagnosis. When Pat came home from the doctor's office, I could tell something was wrong, but I never could have imagined what she was about to tell me. The doctor had diagnosed her as having Huntington's Chorea.

At that time I didn't know what Huntington's Disease was. It is a genetically transmitted disease that involves the premature deterioration of the caudate nucleus of the brain (at the front of one's head). Brain cells simply drop out, and the result is not entirely unlike what happens when an older person shows signs of dementia as a result of aging. Symptoms are both physical and psychological. On the physical side, there is a gradual loss of control of all voluntary body movements. Psychologically, it involves memory loss and depression, and as the disease progresses it can lead to hallucinations and paranoid schizophrenia. Symptoms do not begin until a person is around thirty years of age, though some who have it show no signs of it until their later thirties or even their forties. It is a slow-developing disease, but over several decades it takes its toll, and it is fatal. There are some medications to help with symptoms, but there is no known cure. Only a few years prior to my wife's diagnosis had researchers even discovered the chromosome involved. It was not until 1993 that the exact genetic marker was discovered.

The situation is even worse than that. Huntington's Disease is controlled by a dominant gene. That means that only one parent needs to have it in order to transfer it to their children. Each child has a fifty-fifty chance of getting it, but as mentioned, symptoms don't show up until age thirty at the earliest. We have three children.

Since Huntington's is controlled by a dominant gene, those who have the gene get the disease. If they don't get the disease, they cannot be a carrier. There are tests to determine beforehand how likely it is that one will have it. The accuracy of those tests increased as researchers zeroed in on and finally discovered the exact gene involved. Still, there is a real dilemma over whether to take the test or remain in the dark about one's chances of getting the disease. For example, during one office visit I asked Pat's doctor what was involved in getting tested so I could find out

Prelude to a Problem

what percentage of the cost the health insurance company would cover. The doctor replied that whatever we did, we should avoid reporting any of it to the insurance company. If the test showed that one of our sons would get the disease, it might be impossible for him to get health insurance. It is also possible that an employer would refuse to hire someone known to have the gene for Huntington's. On the other hand, if our children don't know if they will get the disease, they must make decisions about career, marriage, and having children in the dark.

When this news came, my initial reaction was shock and confusion. How could this be happening? Before we were married, we knew that Pat's mother had mental problems. At the time of our wedding, she had been in a mental institution for five years. We asked several people how likely it was that this might happen to Pat, believing all along that it was a purely psychological problem. Psychologists assured us that if Pat were to have such problems, they would have already surfaced. Since she was in her twenties and nothing of that sort had happened, we were led to believe there was no need to worry. We never imagined there was a physiological base to my mother-in-law's problems or that the difficulty could be passed genetically to my wife. Nor did anyone else. Immediate family members knew nothing about this, and others who might have known said nothing. My father-in-law had at one time heard the name of the disease, but did not ask for details about it. Everyone who might have known the truth either didn't know it or withheld the information. Before we started our family, we checked again to see if anything hereditary could be passed on to harm the children. Again, we were assured there was nothing to fear.

We had wanted to discover whether it was God's will for us to marry and later to have children. We told God that we were willing to do whatever he wanted. If he didn't want us to marry, we asked that he would show us that. One way to do so would be to let us learn that Pat would likely get her mother's disease. We searched for this information, but we didn't find it. When we didn't find such information, in addition to other factors that I'll mention later, we were led to believe that God wanted us to marry.

In our thinking, none of this could possibly be happening, but it was. Professionals who were supposed to know about such things had said it wouldn't. I found it all very hard to believe. It was also unbelievable because of the basis of the doctor's diagnosis. He did nothing more than observe Pat's symptoms and then ask about her family history. No genetic tests or tests of any other kind were done that day, but the diagnosis was given. I complained that this was all too inferential. Such skimpy data should not warrant that conclusion. No philosopher would accept that kind of argument. For several months I was torn between the hope that it was not true and fear that Pat's problems could be nothing else. When a second opinion by a specialist doing research on the disease confirmed the diagnosis, all my hopes collapsed.

2

HOW DISMAL
LIFE CAN SEEM

A FTER MY WIFE'S INITIAL DIAGNOSIS AND CONFIRMATION, I was besieged by a host of emotions. Even to this day I wrestle with those feelings. I believe others who experience tragedy undergo similar reactions. If we are to minister to those who are hurting we must understand how they feel. The predominant reaction I experienced was feelings of hopelessness and helplessness. There had been problems before, but usually there was some way out. In fact, I could almost always figure out something to do. But not this time. Huntington's is a disease with no known cure.

I felt that the situation was absolutely hopeless. I would have to watch my wife, whom I dearly love, slowly deteriorate and die. As the disease progressed, maybe she wouldn't even know me. Possibly worse, she would know me, but would turn against me —imagining that I had turned against her. After all, my mother-in-law had misjudged my father-in-law's reasons for putting her in a mental institution for the last years of her life. Eventually Pat would be gone, and yet it still would not be over. The same thing could happen to each of our children. I remember thinking that this threat of doom would hang over me and my family every day for the rest of our lives. There was no morally acceptable way to escape this situation. There was only one person who could do anything about this, and it appeared at that time that God wasn't going to help. Beyond this, it seemed that he had led us into this situation rather than keeping us from it. As I reflected on the hopelessness of our situation, I realized how dismal life can seem.

Beyond the hopelessness, I felt helpless to do anything. I was experiencing physical problems myself that were only aggravated by the stress from this news. Before long I came to a point where I was barely able to do my work. I wasn't much help to my family either. I wanted at least to comfort Pat and help her deal with this distressing news, but all along she has handled this far better than I. Somehow God gave her strength and victory over what was happening, and she didn't seem to need my assistance. I felt locked out of her life at this most critical time, as though I could be of little help. Whatever therapeutic value there might be for me in comforting her was lost.

Though your situation is probably different from mine, I

A Journey Through Suffering

suspect you had similar feelings of hopelessness and helplessness if you have had to deal with some major tragedy. Along with those feelings comes a sense of abandonment. At such times, one feels that there is no answer and no help. Yes, there are friends and family, but what can they do? They aren't miracle-workers. The doctors themselves can't cure this disease. What could others do? Anyway, they have their own families to care for and their own problems to be concerned with.

Something else heightens the feeling of abandonment. Invariably when news like this comes, people are very concerned; but because they are afraid they will say the wrong thing, they tend to stay away. Nobody wants to be like Job's comforters. Better to stay away than take the chance of sticking your foot in your mouth. However, remaining at a distance only confirms the worst fears of the person suffering. One already feels abandoned, and when family and friends keep their distance, they communicate that this apparently is true. The deeper fear is not just that one feels abandoned by family and friends, but that God is no longer there. It doesn't matter how much one has sensed God's presence before, for at times like this, he seems absent. And when one knows that God is the only one who can do anything about the problem, it is especially painful to sense his departure.

These emotions are also accompanied by anger. The anger

may not be particularly rational, but it is nonetheless real. I was angry that this was happening to us. I never expected exemption from problems just because I am a Christian, but I never thought something like this would happen. In one fell stroke we learned that my whole family was under a dark cloud of doom. That kind of catastrophe wasn't supposed to happen. I was angry. Since I had known before I married that God wanted me in the ministry, had we known this about my wife's family, we probably would have agreed not to be married. Pat has said that had she known, she probably wouldn't have married at all. If we had learned of her condition before starting a family, we wouldn't have had children. It is immoral to subject someone to this fate if you know this could happen! I was angry at family members who knew and did not tell us. I was angry at the doctors who knew and never explained it to the family. And I was angry at family members who didn't know even though they could have asked the doctors for an explanation. In short, if someone had told us the truth before we married, we could have avoided this terrible situation.

Though I did not want to admit it, I was also angry at God. I knew that was foolish, because God had not done this. Nor could I think of anything in or out of Scripture that obligates God to keep things like this from happening. Beyond that, it was foolish to be angry at the only person who could do something about this bleak situation. Anyway, who was I, the creature, to contest

A Journey Through Suffering

the Creator? As the apostle Paul says (Rom. 9:19-21), the creature has no right to haul the Creator into the courtroom of human moral judgments and put him on trial as though he had done something wrong. God has total power and authority over me. It was foolish to be angry with the One who has such total control over my every move.

Still, it is human nature to be angry and to expect something different from God. In my case, it was not just that he had allowed this to happen to us. I felt that God had somehow misled me, even tricked me. When Pat and I first met, we were sure there was no way we would marry. I was preparing for a teaching ministry, and she was headed to the mission field. We thought this combination could never work out. Our relationship grew, but I feared that we were in for disappointment if we continued, because it seemed God was leading us in different directions. Before I met Pat I had been engaged to be married. In that case, I had clearly run ahead of the Lord. By God's grace I came to see that, and I broke off the engagement. But the experience emphasized how extremely careful I had to be in choosing a life partner. Above all, I had determined to seek and follow God's leading. It didn't pay to test God by continuing a relationship that seemed outside the divine will.

I sensed that I knew what Pat and I had to do. One night I went to break off the relationship. I was sure God would not want us to defy his will to send us in different directions. As Pat and I talked, we began to realize that she had a definite call to full-time ministry, but there was no clear call to foreign missions. We continued to see each other and prayed about this whole thing, telling the Lord to break it off (as painful as that would be) if he didn't want us together. Rather than destroying the relationship, the Lord made it abundantly clear in various ways that he wanted us to marry. As I grew up, I often wondered if you could be absolutely sure that the person you marry is the right one. I thought that when the wedding day came around, you could be pretty sure you were marrying the right person, but not absolutely certain. That could only come after being married for a time and then seeing that you had chosen correctly. However, in light of how God had so clearly led us, I knew beyond a shadow of a doubt that God wanted me to marry Pat. Indeed, married life has only confirmed that.

With that background, perhaps you can understand why I felt I had been deceived. The Lord knew I was going into a very demanding ministry. He knew that I needed a wife to help me, and he knew that if I were really to give myself to the work he was giving me, I would need at least a relatively healthy wife. My father had a very fruitful ministry of the sort I envisioned. While my mother was never incapacitated to the point that she could not function in the home on a consistent basis, she did suffer with various physical problems—and I knew the strain this placed on my father. I reasoned that God knew all of that, so he would give me at least a relatively healthy wife. Of course, I assumed that the Lord would give me a certain kind of ministry. I couldn't see how I could have a wife with Pat's condition and carry on such a ministry. It didn't occur to me at the time that God might have in mind a different sort of ministry for me. So, if God were thinking what I was thinking, this shouldn't make sense to him either.

I was very confused, and the confusion came in part because the Lord had so clearly led us to marry. Besides, those who had been asked about whether Pat could have the same problems as her mother assured us that there was nothing to worry about. Now I had learned the horrible truth, and I felt that I had been tricked. I had been led down a path, only to learn that I was not getting what I thought I was.

I remember thinking repeatedly at the time that none of this made any sense. God is the supremely rational Being, and yet it seemed that he was actualizing a contradiction in my life! The news of my wife's illness seemed to contradict the Lord's leading in my life over the previous fifteen years. I didn't know what to do, and I didn't even know what to think. At one point, I thought about Abraham. God had given him Isaac, the child of promise, only to tell him to sacrifice his son on Mt. Moriah. That must have made no more sense to Abraham than my situation made to me. Even so, Abraham had believed. He even believed that if he sacrificed Isaac, God would raise him from the dead (Heb. 11:19).

What incredible faith! I should be more like Abraham. Surely his situation should comfort and encourage me. But it didn't. I remembered only too quickly that it made sense for Abraham to believe because God had made very specific promises about this son (Gen. 12:1-3; 15:4-6; 17:15-19). God had made no such promises to me about *my* wife and children. He had made it clear that Pat and I should marry, and even saw to it that information likely to have kept us from marrying and having children was hidden. But he never promised that there would be no catastrophic illness. There had never been any promises about how long or how healthy a life any of us would have. Certainly God could perform a miracle (as Abraham expected in Isaac's case) and heal the disease, but there were no guarantees that he would. As instructive as the example of Abraham and Isaac is, I had no right to take comfort from it.

I was also confused for another reason. I was raised around people who suffered greatly. My mother had one physical ailment after another. I cannot remember a time when there wasn't some significant problem of real and serious concern. I am sure that it was in part because of her experiences that I became inter-

A *Journey Through Suffering*

ested at an early age in the problem of pain and suffering. In addition, both my parents were raised in orthodox Jewish homes. They came to know Jesus as their Messiah and Savior before they married. As you can imagine, with this background they were greatly disturbed by what had happened to the Jews during World War II. I wondered as well how a loving God could allow such a horrible atrocity as the Holocaust. As I grew up, I thought about the problem of evil repeatedly. In seminary, I wrote my Master of Divinity thesis on Job. Later, my Master of Theology thesis was devoted to God's sovereign control of all things and how that relates to human freedom. Then, my doctoral dissertation concerned the problem of evil considered philosophically. If anyone had thought about this problem and was prepared to face real affliction, surely it was I. Yet when the events I have recounted occurred, I found little comfort in any of this intense intellectual preparation.

The truth is, I couldn't figure it out. I had all those intellectual answers, but none of them made any difference in how I felt on the personal level. As a professor of theology, surely I should understand what God was doing in this situation. On the contrary, I began wondering if in fact I really understood anything at all about God. The emotional and psychological pain were unrelenting, and even devastating physical pain resulted from the stress.

Why hadn't all the years of study, reflection, and writing on

How Dismal Life Can Seem

the problem of evil helped at this moment of personal crisis? I was experiencing a religious crisis, and none of this information I had stored away seemed to matter in the least. As I reflected on this, I came to what was for me a very significant realization: All my study and all the intellectual answers were of little help, because the religious problem of evil (the problem about one's personal struggle with pain and suffering and how that affects one's relation to God) is not primarily an intellectual problem. Instead, it is fundamentally an emotional one! People wrestling with evil do not require an intellectual discourse on how to justify God's ways to his creation. Such answers address the more abstract theological and philosophical problems about why there should be any evil at all or evil in the amounts present in our world if there is a God. My problem, instead, was about how in the midst of affliction I could find comfort, and how I could find it in myself to live with this God who was not stopping the suffering.

This does not mean that no spiritual truths or intellectual answers can help the sufferer. It means that many of those answers will not help with this problem and that others that do will not help at all stages in the sufferer's experience. They must be used at times when the emotional pain has healed enough so that they *can* make a difference.

At this point I understood experientially that the religious

A Journey Through Suffering

problem of evil requires pastoral care rather than philosophical discussion. I can illustrate the point by a simple example.

Think of a little girl who goes out to play on a playground. Sometime during her play, she falls and skins her knee. She runs to her mother for comfort. Now, her mother can do any number of things. She may tell her daughter that this has happened because she was running too fast and not watching where she was going; she must be more careful the next time. The mother might even explain (if she knew them) the laws of physics and causation that were operating to make her child's scrape just the size and shape it is. The mother could even expound for a few moments on the lessons God is trying to teach her child from this experience.

But don't be surprised if the little girl responds, "Yes, Mommy, but it still hurts!" All the explanation at that moment doesn't stop her pain. The child doesn't want a discourse; she wants and needs her mother's hugs and kisses. There will be time for the discourse later, but now she needs comfort.

The same is true for each of us as we struggle with the religious problem of evil. When the affliction first comes, we don't want or need a lengthy discourse to appeal to our mind, and that is because this is not primarily an intellectual matter. If someone gives us such a lecture, he or she will find that we are too hurt and confused to absorb it. No, we don't need a lecture! We need something to take away the pain, and a very big part of that pain is not knowing what these events mean about how God feels toward us. Or how we should feel toward him.

3

RECIPES
FOR DISASTER—

Or How Not to Help the Afflicted

———⚭———

I F THE RELIGIOUS PROBLEM OF EVIL (THE PROBLEM ABOUT personal struggles with pain and suffering) is not primarily about justifying God's ways in our world but about how to live with the God who does not stop the suffering, how can we help others through these difficult times in their life? I can only answer in terms of things that were not helpful to me and things that did make a difference.

Invariably, people try to say something they hope will help. Sometimes it does, but often people can be extremely insensitive in the things they say, and this only drives the sufferer into further despair. No one means to do this; no one is trying to make the burden worse. Most just want to help. But despite good intentions, these would-be comforters often wind up doing more damage than good. Let me mention some things that are inappropriate to say.

Recipes for Disaster

"You Must Have Committed Some Sin"

Someone may say, "There must be some great sin you've committed; otherwise, this wouldn't be happening to you." I am very thankful that no one said this to me or my family, though it is a common reaction of some people when they hear of severe affliction. This was the reaction of Job's so-called comforters. They didn't really know what was happening, but they were sure it would not look good for God if a righteous man suffered. Therefore, they reasoned that God would only allow this to happen to the guilty.

While it is true that God punishes sin, and that the wicked will have a day of judgment, Scripture is very clear that sometimes the ungodly *do* prosper (Psalm 73), while the righteous suffer (Job 1:8; 2:3; 1 Peter 4:12-19). The truth is that in most instances we don't really know whether someone suffers as a righteous person or as a sinner. Outwardly moral people may be great sinners, and even those who seem righteous may be guilty of some hidden sin. The story of the rich man and Lazarus (Luke 16) is a vivid reminder that outward appearances do not provide a good basis for judging spirituality. If someone is truly suffering in punishment for sin, that person will likely know it without our saying a thing. If that person doesn't realize it, it is still probably better to ask him what he thinks God is saying through the affliction, rather than offering our opinion that they must have committed some sin. If someone is suffering for righteousness' sake, as was Job, it will definitely not help if those who are not suffering assume an attitude of moral superiority and accuse the sufferer of sin.

Things vs. People

Another mistake is to focus on the loss of things rather than the loss of people. I do not speak from personal experience, but from that of a relative. Some years ago this relative was on vacation. While away, she learned that her home had burned to the ground, trapping and killing her son who was unable to escape. Her pastor tried to be of help but made some significant mistakes in handling the situation. For one thing, he made very little attempt to see her and allow her to talk out her feelings. The few times he did say something, he expressed concern over the loss of her house and possessions. You can imagine how hurt she was. The loss of one's home and possessions is not insignificant, but in one way or another, those things can be replaced. The loss of a loved one is the greatest loss one can suffer, for how does one replace a son? That pastor utterly missed the point of her grief. By his insensitivity, he missed the opportunity to minister to her in her time of crisis and hindered rather than helped the healing process.

"This Has Probably Spared You from Worse Problems"

Sometimes when we lose a loved one, people try to comfort us by convincing us that what has happened is for the best because it spares us from other problems. Here I relate the experience of one of my students. This student and his wife had their first baby, and he was in my class for the term just after the baby's birth. About midway through the term, the baby died very suddenly. After the funeral and toward the end of the term, he shared with the class some of what he had learned. Part of what he told us focused on things not to say to someone experiencing such grief. He told us how some people had said, "You know, it's probably a good thing that your son died. He probably would have grown up to be a problem. Maybe he'd have been a drug addict or would have refused to follow Christ. God knows these things in advance, and he was probably just saving you from those problems."

I trust that no one thinks this is an appropriate thing to say. Maybe that child *would* have been a problem, but it is hard to see how that information is a comfort at the time of loss. Parents and other relatives loved that child, and they loved him regardless of whether or not he was or would have been a problem. Their loss is extremely painful, and the pain is not eased, let alone removed, by insensitive speculations about the future.

Moreover, the comment is wrong, because it in effect says that it is good that evil has happened. I don't see how that can ever be an appropriate attitude for a Christian. Yes, James says we are to count it all joy when we fall into various afflictions (James 1:1-2), but we must not misunderstand this. The affliction is not joy; it is evil. The cause for joy is that in spite of the evil, God is with us and can accomplish positive things in our life even in the midst of affliction. But the affliction is not a good thing. If it were, we might be inclined to seek suffering. Obviously, nothing in Scripture suggests that we should do that. Anyway, we don't have to seek affliction; it has a way of finding us.

"Just Remember Romans 8:28"

It is not unusual for some well-meaning person to see us suffering and offer the following advice. "I can see this is quite a struggle for you. But just remember that in Romans 8:28 God promises that 'all things work together for good.'" Though quoting Scripture to the afflicted can be a good strategy, quoting this passage is not necessarily helpful, for a number of reasons.

For one thing, those who understand what you are saying usually remember that there is more to the verse. Paul says that this will happen to "those who love God, who have been called according to his purpose." It is not unlikely that reminding sufferers of this verse will stir up in them a variety of doubts. They may reason, "Since all things work together for good for those who love God and are called according to his purpose, maybe the reason that this is happening and hasn't yet turned out for good is that my love for God isn't what it should be. Or maybe God has his will and purposes for me, but I'm out of his will, and that's why this has happened. In fact, maybe by quoting this verse my friend is implicitly accusing me of those problems."

Surely, such doubts in no way help the sufferer. The would-be comforter of course does not intend to make the burdens heavier by adding such a burden of doubt and guilt. However, there are other problems with quoting this verse. Clearly, Paul is appealing to the ability of a sovereign God to turn everything that happens to believers, even adversity, into something profitable for them. But in light of verses 29-30, which explain why verse 28 is true, it is clear that the good envisioned here pertains to the believer's salvation, not just anything that contributes to worldly convenience or comfort. Paul writes: "For those God foreknew he also predestined to be conformed to the likeness of his Son, that he might be the firstborn among many brothers. And those he predestined, he also called; those he called, he also justified; those he justified, he also glorified."

Nonetheless, those who quote this verse often think it guar-

A Journey Through Suffering

antees comfort and convenience. If it doesn't, it is simply mis-leading to quote this verse as though it means that the afflicted should feel better because God will soon restore all comforts and conveniences that were lost. That is surely not the verse's point.

There is a third problem with reminding the sufferer of Romans 8:28, especially if one uses it at early stages of the sufferer's affliction. The problem is that it again treats what is primarily an emotional problem as though it is only an intellectual one. We think that if we can just get the sufferer the "right" information, all the pain will just go away. If the mother of the little girl who skinned her knee quoted Romans 8:28 to her daughter, would that remove the pain? Of course not, and not just because she's a little girl!

Do not misunderstand this. There will be a time in the sufferer's experience when it will be helpful to offer this and other theological information in an attempt to comfort. But when emotional and physical pain are so severe, don't expect the sufferer's mind to be functioning at full speed. Even if it is, the right information won't remove the pain!

There are two other problems with quoting this verse, and I think these are the most significant. For one thing, at the point in our suffering when someone quotes this verse, God typically has not brought good out of this evil. Often those who suffer cannot see how or when God will do so. Reminding them of what

God can do before God has done anything is not likely to help very much.

In addition, it is hard to see how that good, whenever it comes and whatever it will be, will make up for the evil that has happened. Surely, the would-be comforter does not mean to say that the evil that has happened is really all right because eventually God will overrule this adversity to do something good! Moreover, I hope that by quoting this verse no one is suggesting that since God will turn things to good, even the evil that has happened is not really evil! Unfortunately, quoting Romans 8:28 may just give the sufferer such false impressions. How insensitive to imply that a tragedy of a lost loved one, or some other tragedy, really isn't that bad or that it is not even evil, because God will eventually bring something good out of the experience! God used the murder of Jesus Christ on Calvary to purchase our salvation, but that doesn't make our Lord's death any less a murder, nor does it mean that those who put him to death deserve praise as moral heroes!

Remember that even Jesus wept when Lazarus died (John 11:35). The fact that Jesus had power to raise his friend from the dead (and did so) did not cause Jesus to think that what had happened was trivial. Jesus knew this was a terrible evil, and so he wept, even though he knew he could raise Lazarus from the dead. Scripture also tells us that as a result of sin, the whole creation was subjected to futility (Rom. 8:20). The fact that God will someday reverse the curse placed on creation (Rom. 8:21) in no way minimizes the evil that has happened. God's overturning the results of the sin in our world and using that to demonstrate his glory and power does not mean the sin was good. After all, God told the human race he did *not* want us to sin. The fact that he can display his mighty and gracious hand in saving sinners does not mean he is actually happy that we sinned, making his salvation possible, or that our sin is not really sin!

Things happen in our world that really *are* evil! Do not minimize that fact by appealing to the sovereign ability of God to bring good even out of the most horrible situation. Somewhere down the road, after the sufferer's pain has somewhat subsided and there has been time to see what God will do in the midst of the tragedy, maybe then it will be a comfort to remind the sufferer of this verse. Don't be surprised if the afflicted person has already recited that verse many times over. Regardless of what good God has brought out of the evil situation, that doesn't mean the evil is not really evil!

"We're All Going to Die Someday"

There are other comments that do not help. Not long after we learned the truth about my wife's condition, someone said this to me: "Well, you know, everyone's going to die from something. You just know in advance what it is in your wife's case."

Even if this were true, how can it be a comfort? Does the thought of your own death bring you comfort? If you knew in advance the *cause* of your own death, would you be inclined to say, "Ah, well, very good; now I can rest easy knowing what will get me"? No one likes to reflect on their own or a loved one's demise. That it will happen to all of us is no encouragement, nor is knowing the manner of our death. That is true even if ours will be an "easy death," not to mention facing death from a catastrophic disease. At the time of someone's grief, do not think you will help them by reminding them we will all die someday, or that at least they know in advance how they will die.

The other problem with this comment is that it is not necessarily true—that is, that we can ever know for certain in advance the cause of our death. Indeed, the likelihood that my wife will die of Huntington's Disease is great, but it is not absolutely certain. She could die of a heart attack, in a car accident, or some other way. None of that is cause for rejoicing either, but it does show that the comment in question is neither helpful nor necessarily correct.

Furthermore, it doesn't help to remind me or my wife that despite her disease and despite the fact that it takes people when they are relatively young, I might still die before she does. That could also be true, but I don't find it comforting to think that at a time when Pat is least able to function and most in need of my help, I might not be there. That doesn't encourage her either.

"Don't Think About Any Major Changes"

When the doctor first diagnosed Pat's condition, he told her some things that he must have thought would be helpful. After giving the diagnosis, he said, "Well, you better think about it long and hard before having any more children. And you and your husband better not think about changing jobs. If you do, you might not be able to get insurance."

I am confident that her physician meant well and wanted to be helpful. Indeed, we needed to think about these things. However, there is a time to be told such things, and right at the outset is not it. Earlier I described the feelings of abandonment and hopelessness. Along with those feelings is the sense that one is trapped in the situation and helpless to escape. What that doctor said in no way helped to alleviate those feelings. On the contrary, it confirmed our feelings of entrapment. While I love my teaching and where I'm doing it, nobody likes to feel that their life's options are being limited or cut off, especially when they face seemingly insurmountable problems.

Yes, we needed that information, but not at that time.

JOHN S. FEINBERG

————— ⊕ —————

Recipes for Disaster

When someone you know gets shocking news, they are in need of some practical advice about their situation. However, timing is crucial. I would encourage you to be ultra-sensitive to their feelings. At the moment when they are feeling totally devastated by the news, don't add to their misery by telling them things that will only add to their feelings of entrapment and abandonment. If you feel you must say something, it would probably be better just to encourage them not to make any major decisions until they have had some time to sort things out. But they probably know that already!

"I Know How You Feel"

One of the most typical things people say is something I have said myself at times when visiting the sick or the bereaved. As we fumble for something to share that will comfort our friend or loved one, somehow it seems appropriate to say "I know how you must feel at a time like this." Through my experiences, I have learned how inappropriate and unhelpful this comment can be. The problem is really twofold. On the one hand, it is not true, and the sufferer knows it. Hence, it sounds phony when you say it. Even if you think you know how I feel, and even if the same thing happened to you, you don't know how I feel and you can't know how I feel. You can't because you are not me

—————⟨∞⟩—————

A Journey Through Suffering

with my particular personality and emotions, with my background and experiences, with my family and the relations we share with one another. Nor can I know exactly how *you* feel when suffering comes your way. Telling me that you know how I feel sounds like an insincere and cheap way to try to comfort me. I know it cannot be true.

If something similar has indeed happened to you, you may tell me this because you think I might be encouraged hearing that others have suffered greatly and yet have survived. If that is your point, then just say that, rather than saying you know how I feel. What you say may still not comfort me, because I may be in too much pain at the time to think I'll ever make it through the particular crisis at hand. You can say this from the vantage point of looking back at your own crisis and seeing that you survived. But remember that I am still in the midst of my crisis. Your experience is no guarantee that I'll make it.

While your reassurance that you and others have survived tragedy may not comfort me, at least that comment is true. You are not telling me you know how I feel when I know you can't know how I feel. You are simply saying that though these things are hard, others like yourself have experienced tragedy and still survived. Unless I am totally different from everyone else, it is possible for me to make it, too.

The other problem with saying you know how I feel is that

49

it really doesn't matter. For one thing, do you think I would rejoice in knowing that you feel as miserable as I do? I would not wish my feelings of grief on my enemies, let alone my friends. To know that you feel as bad as I do would make me feel worse, not better. Beyond that, the fundamental reason it doesn't matter whether or not you know how I feel is that this information alone will not help me. What helps is not knowing you feel like I do, but knowing that you care!

Look at it this way. Suppose some horrible tragedy happened to you. Suppose I had experienced the same thing, and suppose I know you. Now I tell you, "You know, I know exactly how you feel. I've been there myself. But you know what? While I know how you feel, I don't really care about what's happening to you."

Would that comfort or help you? Of course not! However, if I tell you I *don't* know how you feel, but I *do* care, and I want to be of help, that will make a difference. Remember, those who suffer feel helpless, hopeless, and abandoned. They need us to care and to show that care by helping however we can. *They don't need us to share their feelings; they need us to share their burdens!*

It is very important to recognize the difference between "I know how you feel" and "I really feel for you." The former identifies with the sufferer. The latter shows that we care.

DECEIVED BY GOD?

A Journey Through Suffering

"If You'd Just Change Your View of God, Everything Would Be Fine"

As the months wore on after my wife's diagnosis, I longed to have someone to talk to about how I felt. A dear, godly colleague who has been a friend for many years offered to listen. I began to explain how perplexed I was by what had happened. It seemed that God hid information from us about my wife prior to our marriage, and again prior to our having children. I noted that with my Calvinistic conception of God, where God controls all things, this was especially troublesome. Even if I were more inclined toward an Arminian notion of God, where God takes a less active role in the world in order to leave more room for human freedom, it still seemed to me that God should have intervened in our behalf. After all, hadn't we prayed that the Lord would lead us and keep us from making a wrong decision about whether to marry? My friend replied that I was talking about this concept of God and that model of God. What I really needed to do was stop such talk and recognize that God is bigger than all our conceptions of him.

There is something very right about what my friend said. Surely, we can never hope to understand our majestic and mighty God thoroughly through human thought forms. Yet, I found my friend's comments unhelpful. For one thing, he failed to see that his comment about God being bigger than all our conceptions of him is itself another conception of God.

However, the real problem was that my friend in essence was saying that things would be better for me if I just changed my ideas about God. Now, it is true that sufferers who are atheists need to change their perception of God. A Christian who has little training in theology might also need a better understanding of the nature and attributes of God. In fact, even theology professors could hardly be hurt by adjusting their views to a more accurate picture of God.

But even though this is true, there is still a major problem in thinking that this will resolve the religious problem of evil. What is wrong with telling someone in this situation that all they really need to do is just change their view of God? The problem is that this treats a fundamentally emotional problem as if it were an intellectual problem. Please do not misunderstand this. The afflicted *may* have a wrong concept of God, and at some point in dealing with them, we must help them get a better picture of what God is like. On the other hand, if the religious problem is, as I suggest, at root an emotional hurt, that must be handled first. You don't handle an emotional problem by telling someone to adjust their idea of God. You can change your view of God and still find that the pain remains!

There are other forms of this error that are just as common

among Christians. One is, "You know, if you were a Calvinist, you'd see that God is in control of all of this, and then you could rest in him." Another is, "You know, if you weren't so Calvinistic, you wouldn't think God has his hand so directly in everything, and then you'd stop blaming him for what's happened to you." Perhaps the most common is, "When things like this happen, aren't you glad you're a Calvinist? Isn't it great to know that God is ultimately in control of it all, and that he's already planned the way out of your problem?"

The first two of these comments are really saying that this whole thing will be all right if you just change your view of God. We have already talked about this mistake. The third comment doesn't tell sufferers to get a new concept of God but rather tells them to take comfort in their beliefs about God. Don't assume, though, that this will in fact comfort everyone. I am a Calvinist, and I found this comment distressing, not helpful. Because of my belief in God's control over all things, and because it appeared that God had misled me, I took no comfort in the fact that I was a Calvinist. In fact, I remember thinking quite frequently that everything that had happened to me and my family would be easier to take if I were an Arminian. At least then I wouldn't see God so actively and directly in control of what had happened.

What was the problem here? Was it that I really needed to

discard my Calvinism as inadequate? Not at all. Had I been an Arminian, what had happened would still hurt terribly. The problem was that others who made the comment and I as well thought this deep emotional wound could be salved by simply reflecting on this intellectual concept. Indeed, there is a time for explanation and reflection upon what one knows to be true of God. If one's ideas about God are wrong, there is also a time for changing them. But not when the hurt is so deep and so new!

This is not a problem that first requires philosophical or theological discourse; it requires pastoral care. In any given case, no one can predict how long it will take for the pain to subside to the point where the sufferer is ready to think seriously about concepts of God. You can be sure, however, that until it does, it will not help the afflicted to tell them to change their view of God or simply meditate on what they believe about him.

"You Aren't Spiritually Mature Unless You're Happy About This"

There was one other thing I found unhelpful in the midst of this emotional and spiritual turmoil and upheaval. I was concerned about my response to our situation, and I felt guilty that I was not on top of things. After all, Christians are supposed to rejoice in all things and persevere no matter what. Beyond that, as one

A Journey Through Suffering

in a position of Christian leadership, people would be looking all the more closely at me to see how I handled this. Still, I was finding it hard to cope. I preach quite frequently, but for about six months I was physically, emotionally, and spiritually unable to do so. I felt that anything I would say would be hypocritical because I was not living whatever I might preach.

All of this was disturbing enough, but my uneasiness increased. One day I was listening to a Christian radio program. A husband and wife who had lost a daughter in her twenties in an automobile accident were giving their testimony. They recounted what had happened to their daughter and how, as a result of these events, various people had come to know the Lord. They concluded that even though the loss of their daughter was hard, it was all for the best. It was good that this had happened.

I heard that and felt more guilty. It seemed the height of Christian maturity to take life's harshest blow and say that it was good that this had happened. If that is what it means to be victorious in the midst of affliction, I knew I was far from that. I could *not* rejoice over the evil that had befallen and would befall my family. But wasn't I supposed to? After all, doesn't Paul tell us to "give thanks in all circumstances, for this is God's will for you in Christ Jesus" (1 Thess. 5:18)? My sense of inadequacy increased.

What my friend and colleague said on this matter was most

helpful. I told him I knew I was supposed to respond Christianly in this situation. Did that mean, though, that I had to like what was happening? Without batting an eyelash he responded, "You do have to learn to live with this, but that doesn't mean you have to like it!"

This may sound like heresy to some. Popular Christian belief reminds us to rejoice in everything and count it all joy when trials come our way. One is not really "with it" spiritually without being able to say that the affliction is a good thing—or so we are told. I beg to differ. Thinking that way will not help us cope with our grief; it will only add to it as we feel guilty about our inability to do what we think we are called to do.

My friend was right, and I came to see why as I reflected on this over the following weeks and months. First Thessalonians 5:18 is often misread. Paul does not say that we are to give thanks *for* everything, but *in* everything (that is, in the midst of everything). The affliction is evil, not good. Why should I thank God for evil? Furthermore, James 1:2-4 does not say that affliction is good or that it is a cause for rejoicing. It says that we are to rejoice when these things happen because God is sufficient in the midst of trials. We are to rejoice when we face trials because we can see what God is accomplishing *in spite of* the trial. Affliction may serve as the occasion for God to do good things in our life, but the suffering is not good. It is still evil.

A Journey Through Suffering

Because the affliction is evil, I am not required to like it. We live in a fallen world. That is why it is even possible for these things to happen. Scripture is very clear that people die because of sin (Rom. 5:12). If people are going to die, they must die from something, and many will die from diseases that take life. Unless Jesus Christ returns for his church before we die, all of us will die as a consequence of living in a fallen world. If disease and death are ultimately the consequences of living in a sinful, fallen world, how can I applaud it? As a Christian, I am called to resist sin and its consequences in all forms. How, then, can I exult when the consequences of sin befall anyone, let alone a loved one? No, we don't have to like it, and if we properly understand the ultimate cause of disease and death, we had better not like it!

It is wrong in another respect to suggest that the sufferer give thanks for suffering. It is wrong because it ignores our humanness. Grief and sorrow in the face of tragedy are very human emotions. Unless they are admitted and expressed, they will remain inside us and destroy us. Healing cannot come if we deny what we are feeling and act as though it is good that evil has occurred. Those negative feelings must be admitted and expressed. They must be dealt with, not hidden so that the sufferer *acts* as though everything is all right. We cannot help the afflicted if we expect them to deny their humanness.

Realizing that I didn't have to like what was happening

relieved a great burden. Other things helped me as well. Let me turn from things that didn't help to those that did. The things I shall mention didn't all happen at once, and in some cases it took a while after they occurred for their import to sink in. If you are wrestling with the religious problem, I trust that you will read these comments with that in mind. None of it may help you now, but do not hesitate to come back to part or all of it later.

4

THE GOODNESS
OF GOD

—⊛—

THOUGH MANY THINGS DID NOT HELP ME, OTHERS DID. One thing that did help over time came in a conversation with my father several weeks after we first received my wife's diagnosis. I was bemoaning the fact that things looked so hopeless. I couldn't see how I would be able to handle it as Pat got worse. On top of that, there was the prospect of having to go through the same thing with one or more of our children. I didn't know how I would take it. At that point Dad said, "John, God never promised to give you tomorrow's grace for today. He only promised today's grace for today, and that's all you need!"

How true that is! In that one comment I was reminded both of God's grace and of my need to take each day one at a time. God has impressed upon me the fact that I don't have to live my tomorrows today. I don't know how I'll cope when my tomorrows come, but I know that they will come only one day at a time, and with each day, even as now, there will be grace to meet each new challenge—for me and for my wife. That doesn't mean it will be fun, but it does mean that for each day God will provide the strength needed.

As a result of that truth, I began to readjust my focus from the future to the present. I would begin each day asking God for just the grace needed to sustain me for that day. As my prayer was answered day after day, I gained more assurance that God would be there when things got worse. As a result, I found that I worried less about the future and focused more on the present day and its responsibilities.

Another major factor in helping me cope, though I did not realize it at the time, was seeing that God and others really do care. I spoke earlier of the sense of abandonment and helplessness one feels. There is a sense that an incredible burden has been put on one's shoulders, and no one is there to help carry it. In the midst of those feelings, God used various people to show me that he and others knew what my wife and I were going through—and that they cared.

Several incidents in particular were especially meaningful. Shortly after the news came about Pat, my brother Paul came to encourage me. I remember him saying that though I might feel momentarily abandoned, God had not abandoned me, and neither had he nor the rest of my family. At that point I was still in such shock, I didn't recognize that I was actually feeling a sense of abandonment. But God knew it, and he sent my brother to reassure me.

I also remember an important visit from my pastor. No one told him to visit us, and we had not asked him to come. He knew we were hurting, and he cared enough to do something. I remember well the first thing he said to me. He told me that he couldn't begin to know how I felt, but he wanted me to know that he really cared about what was happening, and that he and the church wanted to help in any way possible. This was what I needed to hear. He didn't say much more, but he was willing to be there and to listen. His presence said he cared. At a time when it seems impossible to survive the grief and when everything appears hopeless, we need to know that someone cares and will help.

There were other visits, and words were matched with actions. My pastor noticed that our home was in need of some decorating. He took it upon himself to get together a group of people from the church to do it. It was their way of saying they loved us, were sorry about what had happened, and wanted to do something tangible to express that love. It struck me that this was also God's way of showing me that his people would be there when I needed more involved help to care for my wife.

And now that there is a need for helping Pat with some of the everyday housework, people at the church and other Christian friends are still there showing that they care. Many have given their time and energy freely and sacrificially. What a beautiful picture of God's love for us!

Not only have people at my church been helpful and caring, but so have colleagues and students at Trinity Evangelical Divinity School, where I teach. Students on their own initiative set aside special times each week to pray for us. Colleagues also pray for us and express their concern by asking periodically how we are doing and if they can help.

Those in administration where I teach also showed in various ways that they cared and were willing to help. It was difficult for me to teach my classes for a long time after we first received the news of Pat's Huntington's Disease. Rather than scolding me or threatening to remove me from my teaching assignments, those in administration responded with patience and understanding. I was scheduled for a sabbatical that first academic year when the news came, and I was supposed to work on some writing projects. I was in such physical pain, let alone emotional stress, that I didn't know how I would be able to write during my sabbatical. I mentioned this to the president and dean, suggesting that perhaps I should postpone the leave. They took a more compassionate approach. The president and board told me to take the quarter off, and to consider it a combination sabbatical and medical leave of absence. I was told not to worry about how much writing I would accomplish. Though I did in fact get much done that sabbatical, that fact did not overshadow their care, concern, and compassion toward me at such a difficult time.

All these events and many more convinced me that there were people who actually cared and would be there when things got worse. I also saw these things as God's sign that he cared as well. All of this ministered to me greatly and helped me overcome the feelings of abandonment, hopelessness, and helplessness. I realized through this in an even clearer and fuller way that God did care for me.

There is part of the story I have left out until now. After my wife was first diagnosed, and before we went for a second opinion, we requested a copy of my mother-in-law's chart from the hospital in New York. Because she had died some ten years earlier, and because of my wife's situation, they sent us the chart.

When the chart came, I began to look through it. My mother-in-law had been admitted to that hospital in 1967, five years before my wife and I met and married. As I read the chart, I did not understand all of it, but one thing I saw horrified me. Within a few months of her arrival at the hospital, the diagnosis of Huntington's Disease was recorded in her chart. The information that could have saved us from this situation was there for five years before I even met my wife. The information that could have kept us from having children and saddling them with this burden was right there from 1967 onward. It had been there for twenty years, and no one told us about it, even though we sought answers. When we first learned the truth, it wasn't from that chart.

When I saw that information, I was furious. You can see further why I was so angry and why I felt so cheated and deceived. You can understand as well why comments about it being great to be a Calvinist at a time like this did not comfort me, but repulsed me.

In the months and years that have passed since that revelation, I have come to see this in a different way. For twenty years that information was there, and at any time we could have found it out. Why, then, did God not give it to us until 1987? As I wrestled with that question, I began to see his love and concern for us. God kept it hidden because he wanted me to marry Pat. She is a great woman and wife. My life would be so impoverished without her, but I probably would have missed that blessing had I known earlier. God wanted our three sons to be born. Each is a blessing and a treasure, but we would have missed that had we known earlier. God also knew that we needed to be in a community of brothers and sisters in Christ at church and at the seminary who would love us and care for us at this darkest hour, so he withheld that information, not because he accidentally overlooked giving it to us, nor because he is an uncaring, evil God who delights in seeing his children suffer. I have come to understand that he withheld it as a sign of his great care for us. There is never a good time to receive such news, but God knew that this was exactly the right time.

I have written at length about the need to show those who suffer that we care, because I am convinced this is so very crucial. We must show that we really do care, not only by saying it, but also by showing it through our deeds. Above all, we must not avoid those who suffer. Job's comforters made a lot of mistakes, but there was one thing they did that was very right. When they first heard the bad news, they came to comfort Job and sat with him for seven days and nights *without saying a thing!*

We must be there for those who suffer, if only to listen. It is human nature to stay away, for fear we may say the wrong thing. Be there anyway, even if you say nothing. Your presence and willingness to listen and help say enough. When we keep our distance from those who suffer, we confirm their worst fears that no one cares and that no one will help. Show them that someone cares, not only when the initial shock comes, but in the weeks and months and years that follow. There is a sense in which one never completely recovers from tragedy. The need for the love and concern of others is always present.

In the midst of our problems, I was vividly reminded about how difficult it is to go on with life without hope. I did not really begin to feel much relief from my pain until I began to see some rays of hope. The fact that God and others cared was reason for hope, as was the realization that God would give grace for each new day. In addition, friends who knew about our situation and about this disease could point to specific reasons for hope. For one thing, research on this disease continues. With advances in genetic engineering in the area of gene therapy, there is legitimate reason for hope. It is possible that neither a cure nor even much help will come in time to aid my wife. Still there is reason for hope, because the disease in her case has developed very slowly. Though in recent years her condition has deteriorated more rapidly, she is not as far along as she could be. It is possible as well that in the next few years the deterioration might move more slowly again. As for our children, there is even more reason to be hopeful, for ten to fifteen years in medical science is a long time.

Are these false hopes? I think not. It is crucial that people have a reason for hope. We must not offer false hope, but when there are real grounds for hope we should be quick to point those out. Some of my colleagues are especially sensitive to this need.

DECEIVED BY GOD?

A Journey Through Suffering

When a newspaper or journal article appears that chronicles some advance in research on Pat's disease, no matter how small or insignificant the development, they make a point to show me the article. They realize that it is difficult to go on without hope, so they bring these things to my attention.

Something else that helped me was focusing on the fact that in spite of what has happened, God is good. One particular incident brought that very vividly to my attention. A little over a year after we first received news of my wife's condition, I was being considered for tenure where I teach. In the tenure review interview, I was asked a question that really stopped me in my tracks. One of the members of the committee asked, "In light of what you've been through, can you still say that God is good?" Though I answered affirmatively, I did so somewhat hesitantly. I realized that I had been focusing so much on the problems and on what God *hadn't* done that I really hadn't paid enough attention to all the evidence of his goodness in my life.

In the months that followed, I thought a lot about how many things were going well for us. I believe that no matter how much pain and turmoil one suffers, it helps to focus on the ways that God has shown his goodness. Even if a situation seems absolutely terrible, upon reflection one can probably imagine ways for it to be worse. Counting one's blessings may seem trite, but it does in fact give a different perspective on one's encroaching troubles.

In our case, there were many evidences of God's goodness. For one thing, in its early stages the disease had progressed very slowly in my wife's case. When doctors hear how long Pat has had symptoms, and when they see where she is right now, they find it hard to believe. Because there is no known cure for Huntington's, God is the only one who can do anything about it. I have come to see that contrary to appearances, he *has* been doing something about it. There are no guarantees about its future progression, but I can always be thankful for the extra years of relative normality in my wife's condition.

The love and concern shown to us by other Christians continue, and periodically I am again reminded of God's goodness as I hear of people literally all over the world who have heard about this and are praying for us. In addition, I have often thought that it is a blessing to live at this time in history. During much of the last century (let alone earlier), little was known about Huntington's Chorea. Now it is known that there is a physiological base to this disease, not a psychological one. Moreover, within the last decade or so the chromosome and the exact genetic marker involved have been identified. Scientists and physicians continue to work on combating and perhaps even curing the disease. My wife could have lived at any other time in history and still had this disease. That she and our children live now we take as another sign of God's special goodness to us.

When I look at these and many other things, I can truly say that God has been and is good to us. It is easy to focus on what is going wrong. But when you realize that we live in a world where Satan is so dominant and sin is so rampant, it is amazing that anything ever goes right. The fact that many things do go right is ample evidence of God's grace and goodness to us. Surely, we don't deserve it, and he is not obligated to give it, but he does.

In recent years, I have continually been reminded of 1 Peter 5:7. That verse tells the reader to "cast all your anxiety on him because he cares for you." Usually, we focus on the first part of that verse as we remind one another not to worry about what is happening. The latter part of the verse explains *why* we should do this, and I believe it is most instructive. Peter could have written, "Cast all your anxiety on him because he is powerful enough to do something about it." Or "because he knows the answer to your problems." Either of those thoughts would be just as true as what Peter wrote, but I'm glad Peter wrote what he did. It's as if he was saying, "Of course he's powerful enough and intelligent enough to do something about our problems. He wouldn't be God if he weren't. What we want to know, though, is whether he cares enough to help us. And he does."

Indeed, God does care. Everywhere in our lives, in spite of what may be happening, we can find ample signs that God cares—if we only look for them. God cares because he is so good. Focusing on those truths, as well as reflecting on the many expressions of his goodness, helps sufferers feel more comfortable with God.

5

HIDING
THE FUTURE

—⊕—

I N SPITE OF ALL THESE ENCOURAGEMENTS IN THE MIDST OF affliction, there was still the nagging question of how this could have happened to us. After all, it is not just that my wife is a Christian and has given her life in service to the Lord. The question of why this should happen to her is especially nagging, because it could not be God's retribution for any sin she committed in her life. That she would get this disease was decided the moment she was conceived!

Be Angry at Sin

As I thought about that, I was reminded of an unpopular but very important biblical truth. God told Adam and Eve that if they disobeyed him, they would die (Gen. 2:17). They disobeyed, and the curse fell on them, and the apostle Paul reminds us that it fell on all of us as well (Rom. 5:12). Another way to say this is that Adam's sin and its consequences have been attributed to the whole human race. But if people die, they must die of something. There are many possible causes of death, and disease is one of them. When one realizes this, one understands that though my wife committed no specific sin in her life that brought this disease upon her, this has in fact happened because of her sin in Adam—though she is no more and no less responsible than the rest of us. Of course, that is not the most comforting thought, but it is a sober reminder that this is our fault and not God's. And God did warn us.

The main lesson to learn from this is the enormity of sin and the need to hate it. Shortly after the news came of Pat's disease, I received what seemed to be a rather strange note of condolence from a friend who teaches at another seminary. After expressing his sorrow over the news, he wrote, "I can imagine how angry you must be right now at sin." Frankly, I thought that was a rather odd way to console someone. I knew that sin was the last target of my anger, if it was a focus at all.

And yet as I thought about my friend's comment, I realized he was absolutely right. These kinds of tragic events occur because we live in a fallen world. We may think our sins are a trifling matter. But when one hears the diagnosis of a terminal disease, or when one stands at the grave of a loved one, as we have at my mother's and father's graves over the last few years, one has a vivid illustration of how terrible sin is. God said it would lead to this, but we don't take that warning as seriously as we should unlesss something like this happens.

We may think of sin as trivial, but it is not. We may think the punishment of disease, troubles, and death far outweighs the crime of a little sin. That only underscores how far we are from God's perspective on these things. In light of our relative comfort with sin, a little sin doesn't seem so bad. From the perspective of an absolutely perfect God who has nothing to do with sin, it is atrocious.

Think of it in these terms. If you are a parent, you brought children into the world. You have nurtured them and provided for their needs. You love them deeply, and you express that love in many different ways. In response, you ask that your children obey you, but how do you feel when they disobey? Surely, their disobedience seems far more serious to you than to them. How much more must it hurt God, who has given us so much and who moment by moment sustains us in existence, when we disobey him! We need a different perspective on human sin altogether.

My friend was right. We need to see sin from God's perspective, not ours. We need to hate it. When we see where sin ultimately leads, we begin to understand how truly serious it is, and how much we ought to resist it. I cannot say this will greatly comfort most of us, but it may help to focus our anger in the right direction. It may also help us to feel more comfortable with God as we realize that ultimately we have brought these things on ourselves. God warned us, but *we* wouldn't listen. Thank God that now in our troubles *he* will listen, forgive, and restore!

Help Yourself by Helping Others

Other things helped me cope with our situation. I mentioned earlier that I also had physical problems and that the stress from my wife's news only made matters worse for me. Within a few months I was in great pain and was of little use to anyone. I did not have the physical stamina to preach, nor the energy to make it through my classes. I felt that our situation was helpless and hopeless, and that I was useless and adding to the problem by requiring attention that should have been placed elsewhere. As with many people, my feelings of self-worth are tied in large part to my work and productivity. Being barely able to function made my sense of hopelessness worse.

In the midst of this dilemma, the Lord gave me opportunities to do things to help others. This was just what I needed, because it gave me a chance to get my focus off our problems and onto someone else's needs. Even more, it showed me that I could still be useful. Gradually, as I regained strength and was able to do more, I became increasingly thankful that I could do anything, let alone help others who had shown us so much love and concern.

For those wrestling with some affliction, seek ways to help others. There is therapeutic value in getting your eyes off your problems and in seeing again that you can be of use to others. This helped somewhat to lift my burdens and showed me that when others, including my family, needed me, through God's enablement I would be able to help them.

Where Do We Go from Here?

After many months of grieving and some healing as a result of the things I have mentioned, I began to ask how I would ultimately respond to our problems. I began to consider my options. Would I continue to grieve and fall apart? I had already tried that, and it solved nothing. With that approach, there had been little improvement in my own outlook, and I was of little help to anyone else. I concluded that this approach would in no way solve our problems. My wife still needed a husband, my children a father, and my students a teacher; falling apart wouldn't help any of them. That option seemed a dead end. As Scripture says, there is a time to mourn (Eccl. 3:4), but then one must get on with one's life.

Another option was to get on with my life but exclude God from it. Many people choose this option in the face of affliction. They conclude either that there is no God or that there is, but they will fight him. Neither was acceptable for me. Though there was still some leftover anger toward God, I had seen too many evidences of his working in my life to deny his existence. It made no sense to devote my life to propagating the view that God does not exist or that he is uninvolved with us. Even if that were true, there were surely more productive things I could do with my life.

Rejecting God's existence was totally unsatisfactory, but choosing to fight him was no better. God's goodness throughout my life—even now in this circumstance—did not warrant my turning from him. Even if he hadn't stopped this from happening, he certainly was not the one who had brought this tragedy upon us. Moreover, it is lunacy to pick a fight you can't win. In addition, it is beyond lunacy to fight someone who, rather than being the cause of your problems, is the only possible answer to them.

Another option was to take a leap of faith and trust that somehow this all made sense, though I could explain none of it. In other words, I could simply ignore and bypass the intellect and throw myself on God in the hope that he was there. Some might find that attractive, but it was not a live option for me. It is not my nature to sacrifice the intellect so completely. The questions and the lack of peace would be there until my mind was settled. I did not expect to find all the answers, but I knew I had to find many of them.

The only real option for me was clear—to continue trusting and worshiping God and to get on with my life. I had to stop the seemingly interminable deep grieving and allow emotional healing to continue. I had to focus on answers that would satisfy the emotional dimensions of my struggle and would at the same time give enough intellectual answers to warrant peace of mind. I realized that I could not wait until all those answers arrived to continue with life, for too many people needed my help, and I needed to help them.

As I began to take this approach to my problems (and at some point we all must decide how to respond to our problems), I focused more on the positive things I've already mentioned. The healing and coping process continues to this day, as it will through the rest of my life. I still wrestle with these issues, and there is always great emotional pain as I see Pat's disease progress. But God has allowed me to function again, and there has been progress in dealing with these hurts.

Hiding the Future So We'll Trust Him

God is not only there when the shock of tragic news first comes. At various points along the way when we are ready to hear it, he adds a further word. One of those words of help came from a passage in Ecclesiastes. The passage is Ecclesiastes 7:13-14, and the thrust of it is that God hides the future from us so that we will trust him. The passage reads:

> *Consider what God has done: Who can straighten what he has made crooked? When times are good, be happy; but when times are bad, consider: God has made the one as well as the other. Therefore, a man cannot discover anything about his future. (NIV)*

The context of these verses is significant. The seventh chapter of Ecclesiastes contains a series of aphorisms or dictums, although it is not always easy to see how they fit together. Generally, much of chapter 7 focuses on things that at first appear undesirable in order to show that they do in fact have a certain benefit. The previous chapter shows that things that look good also have a down side. The ultimate message is that we cannot always take things at face value, nor should we think we can always understand them. If this is true of things *we* do and experience, how much more is it true of God and his ways!

A Journey Through Suffering

In verses 13-14 specifically, the author of Ecclesiastes emphasizes the sovereign power of God. Some think the question, "Who can straighten what he has made crooked?" means that if God brings something we consider evil, we cannot make it good (straighten it). Put another way, we cannot overturn God's powerful hand. While this interpretation surely fits verse 14 and its teaching about God's bringing of adversity, I think the writer's point is even more general. That is, just as no one can straighten what God bends, no one can bend what he straightens. No one can overturn what God does; human beings must simply submit to God's providence.

All of this suggests that adversity and prosperity are alike under God's hand. Indeed, the Teacher of Ecclesiastes confirms that in verse 14. God sends both good and bad. He tells us to be happy in the good days. Out of fear over the future, we might be troubled even when things are going well. That worry will help us learn nothing about the future, but it may destroy the happiness of the present.

The writer then says that in evil days, we should "consider." He does not say that in evil days we should be sad, for that comes naturally. Instead, we should "consider." We should think about what has happened, think about the alternation of good and bad, and realize that no one knows when either will come. In fact, what appears to be good may turn out to be evil, and vice versa. Things are not always what they seem.

Why does God give this alternation of good and bad? Why doesn't he always reveal how things will turn out? God does this to conceal the future (so that "a man cannot discover anything about his future"). Why? If we don't know what to expect, we must wait on the Lord to reveal what will come next and entrust it all to him. We may want to change what God will do, but we can't (Eccl. 7:13). We must submit to his providences and simply trust. If we knew the details of our future, we might think we could figure out how to respond to it. We might even think we could change it. In short, we might think there was no need to trust God.

God conceals the future so that we will trust him. You can see how this truth fits my family's situation so well. It was not only relevant before we learned the news that was for so long available but unknown to us; it is relevant now as we contemplate the course of this disease and the future of each of our children.

What are the implications of this truth? If God conceals the future so that we must trust him, does that mean God manipulates people and events so that we will love and trust him? Could it be that he cannot get our love and trust any other way, so he manipulates things to force us to trust him? If that is so, this is

A Journey Through Suffering

no God worthy of praise and worship! Nor is he a good God! This is a conniving, manipulative God who has created us solely for his benefit and really doesn't care about us after all.

As I thought about this, I realized that God is not an evil God at all. By concealing the future, God does make us trust him, but this is compassion, not manipulation. It is compassionate in a number of ways.

Knowing the details of our future would very probably be harmful to us. Suppose our future would be good. No doubt we would be relieved, but the joy of discovery would be gone. What should be great when it happens would lose its excitement as a surprise. We might even be bored, for the joy of anticipation would be gone. Revealing a good future might also make us complacent in our relation to God, and that would be bad. We might conclude that we don't need him.

Suppose our future would be evil. Scripture and common sense teach that the ultimate end of this life is death, and death is evil. If we knew in advance the circumstances of our death, or if we knew what evils would befall us along the way, we might be totally horrified and unable to act as fear paralyzed us. Hiding the future is compassionate because knowing the future would harm us.

Hiding the future is also compassionate because we must not ignore the present, something we might do if we knew the future. If the future is good and we know what it will be, we might become impatient with the present. This sometimes happens to us even without knowing the specifics of the future. When we anticipate an exciting upcoming vacation, we can become impatient with the present. In essence, we overlook the good things that are happening now and lose the present. On the other hand, if our future is evil, we might spend much of our time worrying about it or grieving over our anticipated misfortune. The result in either case could well be a wasting of the present and never really living at all.

One of the things that our experiences have done for me is to focus my attention on the present. I have always been a goaloriented person with a focus on the future. I still plan for the future, but now I plan for the near future and not the distant future. I don't want to know any more about the distant future than I have to. I find myself focusing more on the present and enjoying it more. Some people have encouraged me to join a Huntington's Disease support group. I think doing so would not help me. Hearing stories of other people's symptoms and struggles with the disease would probably cause me to project those symptoms and problems onto Pat's situation. I can easily imagine that once hearing others tell their stories, I would wind up worrying about those symptoms even though Pat might never have them. Thus, I find it easier to cope when I focus on where

A Journey Through Suffering

my wife is today, rather than on what her condition might be somewhere down the road. I don't have tomorrow's grace yet, and I won't need it until tomorrow! We must not be so overly occupied with the future that we lose today. God has hidden the future, so we might trust Him. He is compassionate in doing so.

God also compassionately hides the future because we might foolishly try to change it if we knew it. This is especially true if it is evil; but even if it is good, we might try to change it to make it better. But as Ecclesiastes 7:13 suggests, it is impossible to change what God has decided to do. Why waste the present trying to change something you cannot change?

Another reason God's hiding of the future is compassionate is because we could not handle some of the information about the future if we had it. If the future is evil and if we see it all at once, it could be too horrifying for us to take. On November 4, 1987, I caught a glimpse of the future that just about destroyed me. I am more than willing now to take the future one day at a time. In most cases God compassionately reveals the details of our futures moment by moment, and that is enough. As Scripture says, "Each day has enough trouble of its own" (Matt. 6:34). We don't need to know tomorrow's evil today!

6

GRACE
FROM SUFFERING

—⊕—

A LL OF THESE THINGS WERE SOURCES OF COMFORT AND
encouragement. Yet something was still wrong. There
seemed to be a basic unfairness about our situation. Put simply,
why was this happening to us, and not also to other people?
Wasn't it unjust of God to ask us to bear this burden, especially
when others have trials that are so much less catastrophic? I
believe this is a sticking point for many people that makes it so
difficult for them to live with God.

Please do not misunderstand. I would not wish our pain on
anyone, but it seemed only fair that if others escape, we should,
too. If God could keep others from this fate, why couldn't he
keep us from it? Of course, he owes nothing to any of us *per se*,
but justice seems to demand that we get at least as good a shake
as the next family.

I suspect that most people who experience significant

tragedy in their lives have thought this way at some point. I surely had those thoughts, but I came to see that they contain an error. When philosophers discuss the idea of *justice*, they distinguish between what is called *distributive justice* and *egalitarian justice*. Distributive justice refers to giving each person what is his individual due. If you do good, in strict justice you are owed good. If you do evil, in strict justice you deserve punishment. With distributive justice, each person gets exactly what is deserved. Egalitarian justice, however, is giving everyone the same thing, regardless of merit or desert.

Now I saw the source of the problem. It is not just that sufferers think distributive justice mandates a better fate for them (since they think they have done good). The complaint is that God should operate with egalitarian justice in his handling of the world. We expect him to treat everyone the same, and that means we should escape a specific affliction if others do! Otherwise, it seems that God has been unfair.

Once I remembered the distinction between these two types of justice, I immediately asked why God is obligated to dole out suffering and blessing on the basis of egalitarian justice. Given the demands of distributive justice, all sinners *deserve* nothing but punishment. Why, then, is God obligated to respond to us in egalitarian terms? I could not answer that. If God really did handle us according to egalitarian justice, we would all either experience the same torture or be equally blessed. But those ideas do not match the God described in the Scriptures. It was a tremendous help to realize that part of my anger stemmed from thinking that God is obligated to handle us with egalitarian justice. Once I realized that he has no such obligation, I understood that much of my anger rested on a misunderstanding of what God should be expected to do.

Now this didn't completely solve the problem. Even if God is not obligated to give any of us more than we deserve, and even if we deserve punishment for our sin, still God has chosen to be *gracious* to some. If you are suffering from some affliction, you may feel that God should extend the same grace to you as he has to those who never confront your affliction. God must be unjust, then, for not extending as much grace to you as to the next person.

This objection is very understandable, and I believe that it was at the heart of what was then bothering me. Nonetheless, it is still wrong. The objection now has escalated from a demand that God treat us with egalitarian *justice* to a demand that God grant us egalitarian *grace*.

In two respects this demand is wrong. In the first place, God is no more obligated to give the same grace to everyone than he is to give egalitarian justice to all. He is only obligated to distribute what we deserve. The other point is that since we are talking about granting *grace*, the charge that God has been *unjust* because he gave someone else more *grace* (and this is really what the sufferer is complaining about) is totally misguided.

Grace is unmerited favor, meaning that you get something good you don't deserve. If neither my neighbor nor I merit grace at all (if we deserved it, it wouldn't be grace, but justice), it cannot be *unjust* that my neighbor gets more grace than I. It can only be unjust if God is obligated to treat us with egalitarian grace, and he surely is not. In fact, he is not *obligated* to treat us with any kind of grace. Grace precludes obligation! That's why it's grace and not justice! Hence, it cannot be unjust if someone gets more grace than another. If God graciously chooses to give some of us a better (by our evaluation) lot than others, he has done nothing wrong. We have no right to place requirements on how and when God distributes grace; if we did, that would turn it into justice.

One of Jesus' parables illustrates the point very vividly. It is the parable of the landowner and the workers recorded in Matthew 20:1-16. In many respects this is a strange and difficult parable. It teaches that God has the right to give grace as he chooses, and when he does, no one has the right to envy those who receive God's unmerited favor.

In the parable, Jesus likens the kingdom of heaven to a landowner who went out early in the morning to hire workers for his vineyard. He agreed to pay them a certain wage for the

A Journey Through Suffering

day and sent them off to work. Four more times during the day (each time later than the next) he went out and hired more laborers. The last workers were hired just about an hour or so before quitting time. In none of those later cases did the landowner agree on a specific wage—as he had done with the first workers hired early in the morning. The workers hired later agreed to trust that he would do right by them.

At the end of the day, the landowner called in all the workers to pay them. He began with those hired last and ended with those hired first. What would he pay those hired later in the day? Justice would seem to dictate that he pay them less than what he paid those hired early in the day. But he didn't. He paid everyone the exact wage he had promised to the first workers hired.

The workers hired first complained that this was unfair. After all, they had done most of the work. They had labored through the heat of the day. Why shouldn't they get more than the others? The landowner replied that there was no reason for such anger and envy. Hadn't he agreed to pay them a certain wage, and hadn't he done so? They got exactly what justice demanded. However, there had been no stipulations about the exact amount he would pay the other workers. The only requirement was that he would not do something unjust. As it turned out, he decided to be more than just—he decided to be gracious. Had he done something wrong? Of course not. Whatever was owed, he paid. Out of the goodness of his heart in some cases he gave well beyond anything that was owed.

Should the landowner have done otherwise? Were the workers hired first justified in their anger and envy? The response of the landowner to their protests is most instructive. He asked, "Don't I have a right to do what I want with my own money? Or are you envious because I am generous?" The answer to the first question is yes. If the landowner wants to be gracious with his workers and give them more than they deserve, that is his prerogative. It is his money (his grace), and he has a right to do with it as he chooses. Were the first workers envious because the employer was gracious? Yes, and the landowner's point was that they had no right to be. Nothing they deserved was kept from them; they had no right to envy the grace given to others. Grace is never *owed* to anyone. That's why it is grace rather than justice.

The application of these points is clear. God doesn't owe me exemption from my problems just because he hasn't given you those problems. Giving grace to you does not mean he has been unfair to me. He never obligated himself to give me such grace, so there is no injustice in what he has done (or not done). I have no right to think he has been unjust, for grace is never owed. I have no right to envy you when God has given you a grace he has withheld from me, because he has a right to do with his own grace what he chooses.

Rather than envying the grace given to others, I should be thankful that they have received grace. Surely I would not be happy to see God withhold grace so that others are struck with the same tragedy that has befallen us! Think of it this way. Some of us decided early in life to give up much of what the world counts as pleasure in order to trust Christ as Savior and live for him. Yet others accept Christ late in life, some even while in the throes of a terminal disease. Some may have turned to Christ only after having indulged in all of the pleasures this world has to offer. When we die, each of us will have eternal life. Should I be envious that they received eternal life after a life of indulgence in sin, while I chose to live a life of obedience to God? How foolish such a question is! Would I prefer that God not extend them grace so that they would spend eternity separated from God— just because they accepted Christ late in life? Of course not. I am delighted that our God is so gracious and patient with sinners that he leaves the door to salvation open even for those who repeatedly reject him before they turn to him as Savior. There is no room for envying the grace God gives to others!

This is also true for exemption from suffering. Do not assume that because God has withheld *this* grace from me that he has withheld *all* grace. There are too many examples in my life of God's unmerited favor to think that. Not least among those undeserved blessings are the wonderful wife and children he has given me!

These principles about justice and grace will not likely relieve the pain of suffering, but they can help dissipate anger toward God. I have found them to be liberating, and I frequently remind myself of these principles when I am inclined to lament that God has given others an apparently easier lot than mine.

There is another side to these principles. What if you are the one receiving God's gracious exemption from suffering rather than someone else? Should you feel guilty that others got affliction while you received grace? These questions are even relevant to my family's situation. Earlier I mentioned the dilemma about whether to have our children tested for Huntington's Disease. There are obvious potential problems for those found to carry the gene. But there are also possible difficulties for those who know they will not get the disease. For example, it is not uncommon for those who find that they will not get the disease to feel guilty that they will escape while their brothers or sisters won't.

Viewed in the light of what I have been saying, I believe that no one should not feel guilty for escaping affliction. If what happens were totally a matter of justice, that is, if we all were given exactly what we deserve, then I should feel guilty if you suffer and I don't. But this is not a matter of simple justice. It is a matter of grace. If God in his sovereign wisdom chooses to give you grace, don't feel guilty as though either you or God has done something wrong. Rather, rejoice and praise him for the grace that has spared you the suffering. In addition, feel compassion toward those who have not escaped, and do whatever you can to help them bear their burdens.

If you are the recipient of affliction, never begrudge the grace God gives to others. If you receive God's gracious exemption from suffering, praise him and show compassion to those who suffer. Don't apologize for receiving grace, and don't presume that God's grace means you are better than those who did not receive it. Lastly, don't seek further affliction in order to "even things out" between you and those who are suffering. Affliction will find its way to your doorstep soon enough. Praise God for the grace!

7

USING AFFLICTION
FOR OUR GOOD

———⊕———

I HAVE SHARED SOMETHING OF MY OWN STRUGGLES WITH the religious problem of evil and some of the things that have helped me cope with our family situation. The religious problem is not primarily an intellectual struggle, but rather an emotional one. That does not mean, however, there are no intellectual dimensions to it, for of course what one thinks affects how one feels.

There is another line of intellectual answers that can help in ministering to the hurting. I am thinking of the uses of affliction. Though God is not the author of evil and affliction, he does allow these things to happen. When they do, God is not helpless to use them to accomplish positive things in our lives. While the affliction is not good, it can serve as an occasion for God to bring some good out of what is evil. The fact that God does this and that we can see him working in our lives can reassure us that his hand is still upon us. He is not angry at us, and we are not abandoned. Realizing that God did not bring this affliction but is doing something positive and for our benefit in the midst of it can help us realize that the Creator is good and that he is worthy of our worship.

I want to present a series of things God can do in the life of the afflicted. I have found these principles encouraging, though they were not particularly helpful in the earlier stages of my own struggles. When someone is reeling from the shock of tragedy, it will not likely help to say, "Take heart, there are many positive things God can do through this affliction, and I want to share them with you." At that point, the sufferer is too hurt, too angry, and too much in shock to grasp fully the import of this kind of approach. The afflicted may quickly inform you that they would gladly forgo any of these positive things since they must come through affliction. Or the sufferer may simply ask why, if God can bring good out of evil, he cannot bring good out of good.

Allow the sufferer time to begin healing. At some point later in the healing process, the sufferer will be ready to hear the things that follow.

First, let me be clear about what the following information does not mean. Pointing to. the uses of suffering may appear at first blush to be saying that these positive outcomes are the reasons God allows suffering in the first place. It may even appear that I am saying these uses of suffering prove that God is a good God in spite of the evil in our world.

That is not what I am saying, for I do not believe it to be the case. If that's what I was saying, I would be holding God to be a good God despite the fact that he has not removed suffering and evil because he is able to use evil as a means to accomplish a good end. But to say that is to say the end justifies the means. I do not hold that view of right and wrong, and I do not believe Scripture teaches such an ethic.

This information is not meant to justify God's ways to mankind, the sort of thing Christian philosophers and theologians do when they tackle intellectual questions about why an all-loving, all-powerful God would allow evil in our world. I have addressed such questions elsewhere at length.[1]

There is a difference, however, between justifying God as good in spite of evil and helping the afflicted feel more positive toward God in spite of their affliction. Many things can help remove emotional and spiritual pain as the afflicted seek to live at peace with the God who has allowed this pain. What I offer now is help for healing the breach in the sufferer's relation to God.

How, then, might God use affliction in the life of the righteous sufferer? There are many ways, and I have divided them into ten basic categories. It is natural to think that in any given instance of suffering, God is using it to accomplish only one thing. If we do not immediately sense what that is, frustration arises. However, in any actual case God may intend to accomplish a whole series of things rather than just one, and not just in the life of the sufferer alone. God may intend to accomplish something in the sufferer's life, something in the lives of those who know the sufferer, and something in regard to angelic and demonic forces. A particular case of suffering may have several uses of affliction at work.

What possible good might God accomplish in our lives through the afflictions we undergo? First, God may allow affliction for the same reason he had in the case recorded in John 9:1-3. In that situation, affliction provided an opportunity for God to show his power. In John 9, the disciples asked Jesus about a man blind from birth: "Who sinned, this man or his parents, that he was born blind?" Jesus rejected the common belief that all suffering must be a punishment for some specific sin. He answered instead, "Neither this man nor his parents sinned; but this happened so that the work of God might be displayed in his life." To the amazement of those who saw it, Christ then performed a miracle to restore the man's sight. Similarly, God sometimes allows affliction in the life of the righteous as a basis for some future work that demonstrates his power and glory.

A Journey Through Suffering

To some extent, we have seen this happen in my wife's case. Though there is deterioration in her condition, doctors repeatedly mention how wonderful it is that the disease has progressed so slowly for so long. On more than one occasion we have used those comments as an opportunity to state our belief that we are not just lucky. Rather, this is evidence of the hand of God in her life. Even though deterioration has been more rapid over the last year or so, that cannot negate the display of God's power in Pat's life in the early stages of this disease.

Second, God may use affliction to remove a cause for boasting. When things go smoothly in life, we tend to feel self-sufficient. Affliction reminds us that we aren't, and that we must ultimately rely on God. A classic illustration of this principle comes from the life of the apostle Paul. Paul had a thorn in the flesh, some sort of physical ailment whose exact nature commentators debate. In 2 Corinthians 12:8-9, Paul says he pleaded with God to remove the thorn, but he did not. Paul then wrote that if God had removed the problem, he might have thought too highly of himself in view of the significant revelations God had given him. His thorn in the flesh was a constant reminder that there is no room for boasting. Sometimes God uses affliction similarly in our lives.

In the first two chapters of Job, we see a third way God uses the suffering of the righteous. God allowed Job's afflictions at

Using Affliction for Our Good

least in part to demonstrate genuine faith to Satan. Satan claimed that the only reason Job served God was that it was worth Job's while. If God removed his hand of blessing from Job, the servant would no longer serve. God answered that Job served him out of genuine love, and he decided to prove that to Satan. Through Job's afflictions and through his faithfulness to God, Satan saw that there are those who actually do serve God out of true love, not because "it pays to do so."

God may use affliction in our lives to accomplish some purpose *for us,* and at the same time use our response to show Satan and his legions that there are still those who love and serve God regardless of their personal circumstances in life. Others will see this as well. This is extremely important, for as Christians we claim to have the ultimate answers to life's problems. Of course, it is relatively easy to be a Christian when everything is going well. What many non-Christians want to know, however, is whether Christianity works when things go wrong. That's one of the true tests of any religion. If we turn from God in the midst of affliction, we communicate to those watching that Christianity offers no more of an answer than any other religion or ideology. God still needs people today who will show others that even when life brings the unexpected and the tragic, they will continue to love and serve God, not because it pays to do so, but because he is worthy of devotion.

A Journey Through Suffering

This is why Peter tells us that in the midst of affliction we must be ready to explain why we continue to hold on to our hope in God (1 Peter 3:15). This verse is frequently taken out of context to show that Christians should always defend the faith in general. That is neither the point nor the context of the verse. Peter is discussing the suffering of the righteous. He says that when suffering comes, and we are challenged to explain why we continue to trust God and remain faithful to him in spite of what has happened, we must be ready to defend our continued belief in God. Our response must be both verbal and non-verbal (1 Peter 3:15-17). We must not only explain why we have hope and why Christianity makes a difference, but we must live as people for whom Christianity makes a real difference. We dare not use our affliction to justify deserting Christian principles and disobeying God's word.

Fourth, sometimes God uses affliction as an opportunity to demonstrate to believers and non-believers the concept of the body of Christ. According to 1 Corinthians 12:12-26, each believer in Christ as Savior is a member of the body of Christ. As Christians, we are related to one another through Christ, and we need one another. Moreover, verse 26 says, "if one part suffers, every part suffers with it." That means that when one suffers, all suffer, and when one rejoices, all rejoice. This is the ideal, but it does not always match our experience. Too often Christians treat one another as if there were total isolation among members of the body of Christ. To correct this mistaken attitude, God may on occasion use the affliction of one member of the body to show other members that believers need each other and must help one another.

Through affliction the body of Christ concept may be demonstrated in several different ways. Suffering gives opportunity for afflicted people to experience the compassionate love of God through other believers. It allows sufferers to understand experientially what it means to have their burdens carried (Gal. 6:2). As I have already mentioned, these truths have been vividly reinforced to us on many occasions through the words and deeds of other believers who care.

In addition, suffering gives other believers the opportunity to express Christian love to those in need. When we help afflicted members of the body, we understand more fully how deeply we need one another. We experience as well what it means to show Christian love and compassion. In order to give us that opportunity to minister, God may allow affliction to strike another member of our spiritual family.

Jesus said that people would know we are his disciples if we love one another. Helping a suffering brother or sister is a tangible way to show that we are followers of Christ.

These are only some of the uses of suffering, for there are

others. Next I want to examine the relationship between suffering and personal holiness. As we shall see, there are many ways that God can use suffering to help us turn from sin and become more like Christ.

8

SUFFERING
AND HOLINESS

—⊕—

S CRIPTURE TEACHES THAT IN A NUMBER OF WAYS AFFLICTION
in the life of the righteous promotes holiness. First Peter 4:1-
2 makes the general point that the experience of suffering helps
the believer to put away sin. Peter writes:

> *Therefore, since Christ suffered in his body, arm your-*
> *selves also with the same attitude, because he who has*
> *suffered in his body is done with sin. As a result, he*
> *does not live the rest of his earthly life for evil human*
> *desires, but rather for the will of God.*

When Peter says the sufferer "is done with sin," he is not
saying that by suffering the believer is completely removed from
the power, influence, or guilt of sin. As 1 John 1:8 suggests, "If
we claim to be without sin, we deceive ourselves and the truth
is not in us." It is impossible to remove sin's influence com-

pletely in this life. Instead, Peter means that afflictions have a way of driving believers away from committing specific acts of sin. They do so by helping us resist the temptations that surround us rather than yielding to them.

I have found this to be true in my own experience. In light of my family's situation, certain things that enticed me before pale in significance to the ultimate issues of life and death. That is not to say that those things never tempt me or that I never sin. Rather, what has happened to my wife and family has helped tremendously to put those temptations in proper perspective. Life is not about such enticements; much more important things are at stake. When affliction drives us from committing specific acts of sin, we draw closer to the Lord and view things more with the significance that he puts on them. This is evidence of the Holy Spirit at work in us to help us grow in holiness and conformity to the character of Jesus Christ.

Another way affliction promotes sanctification is by refining one's faith. First Peter 1:6-7 says,

> *In this you greatly rejoice, though now for a little while you may have had to suffer grief in all kinds of trials. These have come so that your faith—of greater worth than gold, which perishes even though refined by fire—may be proved genuine and may result in praise, glory and honor when Jesus Christ is revealed.*

A Journey Through Suffering

The focus of this test of faith is not on the test itself, but on the outcome of the test. That is, the focus is the residue of faith that remains when the test is over. Peter's point is not that the test itself is precious, for the test is suffering, and that is not more precious than gold. Rather, the faith left after the test is precious. Therefore, as Peter says, believers can rejoice in the midst of affliction because through these experiences God is refining their faith. The ultimate result is that at Christ's appearing the believer's tested faith will be found genuine and will result in praise and honor and glory.

Holiness is also promoted by suffering, when God uses it to educate believers in ways that cause them to grow closer to the Lord and to be more Christlike. For example, James 1:2-4, Romans 5:3-4, and 1 Peter 5:10 teach that God develops perseverance or endurance through adversity. Hebrews 5:8 indicates that even Christ in his humanity learned obedience through suffering. Now, if God is to teach us anything, he must have our attention. When there is no affliction in our lives, it is easy to become overly self-sufficient and inattentive to what he wants to teach as he desires to draw us closer to himself. When affliction comes, though we may be inclined to rebel against God, if we pay attention to what God is trying to teach us, we may instead learn things we might not have been otherwise open to hear.

Through difficult experiences believers can also draw closer to the Lord by catching a glimpse of his sovereignty and majesty such as they have never seen before. Job 42:2-4 records the response of a man who had suffered as much as any man has ever suffered. Even though Job was righteous (Job 1:8, 21-22; 2:3, 10), he still passed through great pain—and he sought God to understand why. The Creator finally answered Job (chapters 38-41), overwhelming him with a sense of his power and majesty. Job exclaimed (42:2-4) that he now understood God could do anything. In our case as well, sometimes our view of God is far too small, and God expands that view by sending afflictions and proving himself to be the all-powerful One on our behalf. Like Job, we draw closer to the Lord as we come to know him better.

Suffering also produces sanctification because it leads to intimacy with God. Again Job's case is instructive. Even though Job had grown in the Lord before his suffering, he needed to draw closer. At the end of his ordeal, his comments show he had come to know God deeper than he had ever known him before. He says, "My ears had heard of you but now my eyes have seen you" (42:5). Job's mere hearsay knowledge became firsthand experience. There is nothing like affliction to change intellectual abstractions about God's sovereignty, comfort, and concern to concrete realities.

Affliction can stimulate sanctification in yet another way. God may use it to challenge the righteous to growth, instead of falling into sin. This point arises from James 1:1-12. There, the topic is clearly affliction, whereas later in James 1 the topic is temptation to sin. The typical Greek word for tribulation, affliction, or suffering is *thlipsis*. *Thlipsis* never appears in the New Testament in a context where it means temptation. On the other hand, the noun *peirasmos* and the verb *peirazo* are the usual words for temptation and to tempt. In several verses, they indicate a trial or testing (cf. 1 Peter 4:12; Acts 9:26; 16:7; 24:6; Rev. 2:2, for examples). However, those verses do not emphasize affliction or suffering, but rather putting someone to a test.

In light of these basic New Testament uses of *thlipsis* and *peirasmos*, we would expect to find *thlipsis* in James 1:1-12 and *peirasmos* in verse 13 and following. Instead, *peirasmos* is used throughout the chapter, and *thlipsis* does not appear at all. This leads me to ask the following questions: Is James suggesting that afflictions are temptations or trials? Are all temptations afflictions? Are all afflictions temptations?

The answer to the first question is debatable, but the second and third questions are easier to answer. Are all temptations afflictions? Obviously, they are not. Some temptations come in the midst of afflictions (for example, the temptation to curse God that confronted the afflicted Job), but many times temptation arises without any accompanying affliction at all.

Are afflictions temptations? All afflictions are potentially temptations because they provide an occasion for us to be tempted. For example, when one is angry at God, one is tempted to turn from him. We may yield to that temptation, but we may instead respond positively in faith and resist the temptation that came from our troubles. When we do resist, the affliction serves as a basis for growing closer to the Lord. Perhaps this is implicitly James' point in using *peirasmos* when the term *thlipsis* would seem to be the more natural choice of words.

A final way adversity promotes holiness is by offering sufferers the opportunity to imitate Christ. Many would love to imitate Christ if that meant having his power, glory, and authority over all things. We are called, however, to imitate Christ in other ways. Those who suffer for righteousness may suffer unjustly and for the sake of others. In so doing, they imitate the Savior's example (1 Peter 3:17-18). Moreover, those who suffer as righteous may be required to bear that affliction and persecution without complaint. In doing so, they again follow the Lord's pattern (1 Peter 2:23).

Jesus put in perspective the whole matter of what his disciples should expect. He said, that "a student is not above his teacher, nor a servant above his master. It is enough for the student to be like his teacher, and the servant like his master" (Matt. 10:24-25). If the disciple is to be like his teacher, and if his teacher is Jesus, the disciple can expect to get from society the same thing Jesus did. The people of his own day nailed our Lord to a cross. Can Christian disciples realistically expect to escape persecution?

The apostle John confirms this point as well. He tells us that the children of God can expect their goals, values, and lifestyle to be misunderstood by those outside of Christ, and for the same reason that Christ was misunderstood (1 John 3:1). The world did not share or understand the Lord's goals and values. The result was that his enemies put him to death.

The more Christlike we become as children of God, the less we can expect to be understood and accepted by the world about us. And the more we can expect to incur the wrath of Satan and the world. Of course, as we imitate Christ in his sufferings, our sanctification or holiness is promoted.

All of this means that even in the midst of the worst affliction, God is at work to use suffering to draw us closer to him. That does not make the grief and pain any less evil, but it should encourage us to realize that affliction is not a sign that God has turned away. Rather, he is using the pain and suffering to stimulate our growth in Christ.

9

FROM PAINFUL TRIALS TO POSITIVE TESTIMONY

———∞———

SOME SUFFERING MOVES BEYOND THE GENERAL CATEGORY of sanctification, where God uses it to prepare us for future ministry and blessing. For example, sometimes God permits affliction in the life of the righteous for the ministry that is possible in suffering. There are several ways afflicted believers can minister in spite of and even because of their distress. Those who experience adversity can have a tremendous testimony to those who do not know Christ as their personal Savior. Many non-Christians watch very closely how Christians react when they go through troubles. When they see the righteous experience affliction and remain faithful to the Lord, they are positively impressed. As Peter says (1 Peter 3:15-16), their persevering faith and the positive testimony it gives not only puts to silence the negative thoughts of evil men, but also serves as a positive witness to those who do not know God personally through Christ.

—— ⊕ ——

From Painful Trials to Positive Testimony

Just as suffering provides a testimony to non-Christians, there is a ministry to Christians as well. Those who remain true to the Lord during hardship serve as an encouragement to others to remain faithful in spite of their own problems. Moreover, God uses suffering to prepare us to comfort others who undergo troubles (2 Cor. 1:3-4).

There is also a sense in which those who remain loyal to God in the middle of trials are actually ministering not only to others but to themselves. That is, as we cling to God in our suffering, he uses this to prepare us for even greater ministry. Here I think of the role affliction played even in the life of Christ to prepare him for further and greater ministry. In Hebrews 2:10 we read, "In bringing many sons to glory, it was fitting that God, for whom and through whom everything exists, should make the author of their salvation perfect through suffering."

The words "make perfect" do not refer to sinless perfection. That would make no sense in this case, for Christ has always been perfect! Instead, the words mean "to be brought to completeness or maturity." In other words, Jesus Christ in his humanity was prepared to be the complete Savior (everything a Savior should be) by means of enduring various afflictions, even before he went to the cross. If God could use adversity to prepare Christ to be our Savior, surely he can use suffering to prepare us for greater ministry.

A Journey Through Suffering

God also uses pain and distress to prepare us for further trials. Just because one difficult trial hits us, that is no reason to think we have had our lifetime quota. Since we live in a fallen world, we can expect to face further affliction. In fact, there may be even greater and more severe trials yet to come. Had they come sooner, perhaps they would have destroyed us; but God in his goodness and grace prepares us for each new test. Part of that preparation involves confronting and enduring current pains and sorrows.

Think of Abraham. Suppose that in his *first* encounter with God he was required to offer up his son Isaac (Gen. 22). No doubt that would have been too much for him. God knew that, so he did not give Abraham the most difficult trial until he had brought him safely through others. Faith and endurance, like other Christian virtues, can grow and develop. One of the ways God helps those virtues grow is by sustaining us successfully through our present trials. He knows exactly how much we can endure at any given moment. Part of God's program of giving us grace to endure each day is to prepare us to receive and use tomorrow's grace when we face that day's challenges.

Another general use of suffering in the lives of the righteous is to prepare them for the judgment of their works. According to 1 Peter 1:7, affliction helps prepare the believer for the coming of Christ. After Christ returns for the church, all believers will give Christ an account of what they have done in their lives (1 Cor. 3:10-15; 2 Cor. 5:10). In 1 Peter 1:7, Peter says that affliction helps prepare sufferers for that judgment so that their faith and actions will result in praise, glory, and honor when Jesus Christ is revealed.

The connection between suffering and reward may be unclear, but it can be explained. As we endure afflictions, we should become more Christlike, leading to lives that are likely to be filled with deeds that please God. At judgment time it will be evident that we have built lives of gold, silver, and precious stones, not ones of wood, hay, and stubble (1 Cor. 3:12-15). There will be rewards for lives pleasing to God. So, rather than interpreting hardship as a sign of God's displeasure, we should realize that God may be using it to prepare us for the day of judgment when our endurance under fire serves as the basis of reward.

Moreover, God may use our afflictions as a basis for ultimately exalting us. Peter repeatedly teaches the theme of suffering and glory (1 Peter 1:6-7, 11, 21; 2:12, 19-21; 3:9, 14-22; 4:1, 4, 12-16, 19; 5:1-6, 9-10). The message is quite clear: Those who would be great in God's economy must first be brought low. Peter writes, "Humble yourselves, therefore, under God's mighty hand, that he may lift you up in due time" (1 Peter 5:6). Affliction certainly helps to humble us, but regardless of how much we are humbled, suffering endured for righteousness' sake is clearly a prelude to exaltation. A beautiful example of this truth is Christ himself (1 Peter 2:22; cf. Phil. 2:5-11). If we are finally to reign with Christ, we must follow his example of righteous suffering.

Finally, God may use our burdens and oppressions as a means to take us to be with himself. As life comes to an end, our final affliction will usher us into God's presence. This may not seem like a positive thing, but that may be because we do not fully agree with Philippians 1:21, "For to me, to live is Christ and to die is gain." I am not suggesting that we should wish to die, or that death itself is good. The reason for death (sin) and the event itself are not good. But for the believer, death is the doorway to everlasting blessing in the presence of God. Therefore, the death of a Christian believer is not necessarily a sign of God's displeasure. Affliction leading to death may well be God's way of promoting someone into his presence.

This completes my list of the uses of suffering. In a given instance, one or more of these may explain in part God's reasons for allowing evil to befall his people. Perhaps he is doing none of these things in a particular case. But when someone experiences affliction and is angry that God does not stop it, I believe that pointing to these uses of evil can often help relieve the sufferer's feelings of confusion and anger. Of course, sometimes it is impossible to determine exactly why God allows suffering on a particular occasion. God may simply want to remind us that his ways are ultimately beyond our scrutiny. At some point we all need to let God be God and know a few things we don't!

Sufferers may wrestle with a further question. The uses of suffering show that God is able to bring long-range good out of short-range *evil*. But isn't an all-powerful God also able to bring long-term good out of short-term *good*? If he can, why doesn't he? Scripture does not give us the answer, and I am not sure that we can know the answer for a certainty until we stand in the Lord's presence. I can, however, make a suggestion about what may in part be God's reason for not using short-range good to bring long-range good. My suggestion is this: God wants to work in our lives to accomplish his good purposes. In many cases, as we have seen, he wants to teach us something. But it is very hard to teach someone anything unless you have their attention. Affliction has a way of getting our attention like nothing else. Yes, God could bring long-range good out of short-term good, but when we experience nothing but blessing, we tend to be overly self-confident. We might not pay attention to God. If so, whatever else God wants to teach us through the experience will likely be lost.

Is this always the reason God brings long-term good out of short-term evil rather than out of short-term good? Only he knows for sure. But at least this suggests a possible reason for God's accomplishing his goals by means of suffering.

Often we do ask God to keep us from hardship and affliction. When that doesn't happen, it is easy to become angry and to wonder why God doesn't respond. On the other hand, if we take seriously the fact that our world is fallen and that we are engaged in a spiritual war, we realize better why God does not always end our suffering. Better than requesting exemption altogether from the battle and from the wounds that come with it is the taking of Phillips Brooks's wiser counsel:

> Do not pray for easy lives; pray to be stronger people! Do not pray for tasks equal to your powers; pray for powers equal to your tasks. Then the doing of your work shall be no miracle, but you shall be a miracle. Every day you shall wonder at yourself, at the richness of life which has come to you by the grace of God.

10

DECEIVED
BY GOD?

———⊕———

I T HAS BEEN NEARLY A DECADE SINCE THAT FATEFUL DAY
when we first received the shocking diagnosis of Pat's condition. Though the stress and pain that first beset me have greatly
subsided, they are not completely gone. As Pat's condition gets
worse, there are new frustrations and new sorrows as well as
new battles to address in dealing with the symptoms of Huntington's Disease.

If Pat were gone, however, that would not remove the
pain. It would just add another reason for the tremendous hurt.
Every now and again I hear of someone whose wife or husband
died very suddenly. At times I have asked myself whether it
would have been easier to lose Pat all at once or slowly, as is happening. Though I would want neither of those options, I have
come to the conclusion that God is gracious in what he has
allowed to happen in our case. I do not enjoy seeing what is hap-

pening to Pat, but even having my wife at two-thirds or one-half of what she was is better than not having her at all. Still, whatever path God chooses for each of us, we know he will give the necessary grace to walk it.

In spite of all the lessons I have learned through these experiences, and in spite of all the sources of encouragement I have recounted, for many years I found especially troubling not just what was happening, but how it had all come about. This is surely not a life I would have chosen. As I have shared, one of the most difficult things isthat it appeared I did have a choice, for I didn't have to marry Pat. Once we married, we did not have to have children. It seemed, however, that I made those choices under false pretenses. I was led to believe by God, or so it seemed, that I was choosing one sort of life, when in fact I wound up with exactly the life I was trying to avoid. In fact, I was saddled with a situation worse than anything I could have ever dreamed in my worst nightmare.

For a long time I was hurt and anguished by the thought that somehow God deceived me into marrying Pat by hiding information that could have saved me from my present circumstances. There were also questions about knowing and doing God's will. Was it really not God's will that I marry Pat and that we have children? Could I have been that mistaken about God's design for my life? Or was it really God's will that I marry her, but when one follows the Lord's leading one can expect to be double-crossed?

Such thoughts are among the most disturbing of all that have besieged me over the years, and they have been as disruptive of my relationship with the Lord as anything that I have ever experienced. I was raised in a home where a high premium was placed on telling the truth. If our word cannot be trusted, what are we really worth? This is part of the very core of my outlook on and approach to life. How utterly distressing, then, when God, the very embodiment of truth, appeared to have deceived me!

In spite of all the other spiritual truths I have learned, I knew I would still feel uncomfortable with God until I sorted all this out. After many years of wrestling with these questions, and after most of my feelings of anger toward God were gone, I have come to terms about whether or not I was deceived.

Was I deceived by God? I have come to see that I was in fact deceived. But I was not deceived by God. Though it is hard to accept blame for such a critical error as this, I see now that I was deceived by myself. Given my background and the circumstances surrounding my meeting and marrying Pat, I constructed a case for a life relatively free of troubles. But that wasn't the only possible conclusion to infer from God's leading me to marry Pat and start a family. Let me explain.

JOHN S. FEINBERG

Deceived by God?

My mother's illnesses and the strain they placed upon my father and his ministry made me conclude that anyone embarking on such a ministry would be best able to fulfill that work with a healthy wife and children. I knew that God was calling me to a life of scholarship, preaching, and teaching. I reasoned that whomever God would have me marry would be healthy or at least not so unhealthy as to jeopardize the ministry God was giving me. All of this seemed logical and reasonable enough.

I approached dating and marriage armed with such a mind-set, a very natural thing to do. Someone raised in the home of an alcoholic, for example, would be very smart not to marry an alcoholic themselves. I knew it would not be impossible to minister effectively if I had a wife whose health was poor, because I had seen my father do it. But it would be easier to minister without such a hindrance. God knew that, and so did I. I concluded, then, that if I was careful about such matters, God would probably not lead me to marry someone whose health would stand in the way of the work he had given me to do.

When Pat came into my life and we began to get serious about one another, we were very concerned about disobeying God's will. It was not the matter of her health that troubled us at that point, but rather the apparently incompatible forms of ministry to which we thought God was calling us. God resolved that issue, however, in a way that neither of us originally expected, showing us that we could minister together without contradicting his will for our lives in the slightest. The only other question concerned Pat's health, but it was exceptionally good at that time. There were no signs of what was to come, and we were assured that what had happened to her mother would not be passed to Pat.

My love for Pat, my belief about the need to have a healthy wife, my assurance that Pat would not get her mother's disease, and the clear leading of the Lord concerning our respective ministries led me to conclude that God wanted us together. Though such thinking is sound, it is still a clear example of inferential reasoning.

Inferential reasoning is reasoning from things that are clearly known to a conclusion that is not known but seems necessitated by the things we do know. For example, Scripture clearly teaches that there is only one God. Just as clearly, however, it refers to three distinct persons (Father, Son, and Holy Spirit) as God. From such clear biblical truths, Christians throughout church history have concluded that the right way to think of God is as triune. Nowhere in Scripture do we find the word *Trinity*, nor does any passage say that God is one as to his essence or nature but three as to the manifestations of that nature. Nonetheless, such a doctrinal conclusion seems inevitable on the basis of what Scripture clearly teaches about God.

JOHN S. FEINBERG
———— ∞ ————
Deceived by God?

Although the inference to the doctrine of the Trinity is a natural and accurate inference, and although that doctrine is certainly taught in Holy Scripture, inferential reasoning is notoriously risky. From precisely the same information, it may be possible to draw several conclusions. For example, from the fossil records the atheistic scientist concludes that evolution is correct; but from the same data, the Christian scientist finds scientific support and evidence for a Creator. How can this be since the "facts" are the same for both the Christian and non-Christian? This shows just how tricky inferential reasoning can be.

So it was in my case. From my reasoning about needing a healthy family in order to be free to minister, from the information we had at that time about Pat's health and the health of her family, from the Lord's leading regarding our respective ministries, and from the love he placed within us for each other, it was thoroughly logical to infer that we should be married and that health would not curtail us. What I have come to see over the last few years is that while such inferences were natural ones to make and could have been correct, they were not the only ones that were possible from the data we had. The conclusions I reached were reasonable, and they surely matched what *I* wanted to happen. But our best-case scenarios do not always match what God has planned for us, even when we think we can build a rational case that things are going to turn out just the way we want.

So where was the mistake in my thinking? Had God actually deceived me? Or had I mistakenly drawn the wrong inference from the information I had? I was certainly not wrong about my love for Pat, or hers for me. Nor was I mistaken that God wanted us to marry and minister together. I didn't have all the information I now know about Pat's health, but is God to be blamed for that? He could only be blamed for not giving me the pertinent information if he was *obligated* to give me that information before we married.

Yet, what could possibly place God under such an obligation as that? For a long time I thought that the need for my wife to be healthy in order for me to accomplish my ministry was enough to obligate God to inform me about the potential health risks of a prospective mate. That belief made me infer from the facts as I knew them at the time not only that I was to marry Pat, but also that she would not have any major ongoing health concerns.

In believing all of these things, I deceived myself into thinking I was getting a different life than I have. Having called me to the ministry and having led me to Pat, God was only obligated to inform me of her medical history before we married if it would be impossible to carry on his work with a wife in poor health. In fact, it is not. From my dad's case, I knew that it was preferable for someone in ministry to have a healthy family. I also knew from his case that it is *possible* to minister very effectively even if your wife or other family members are in poor health. Moreover, I have come to see that God's intended service for Pat and me is a bit different than we anticipated, and it is service we can do on behalf of the kingdom even though she has this serious illness!

The truth is that God had never promised me anything about my wife's health. I simply saw what I thought would be preferable for someone like myself, and I wrongly concluded that God would agree. It made logical sense, but it was not accurate.

Yes, I was deceived, but not by God. He didn't tell me anything that was false, nor did he mislead me. He was not obligated to inform me before we married that Pat was even at risk for Huntington's Disease, let alone that she would get it.

I have written much about being deceived by God. I have done so for several reasons. For one thing, it is such an important part of my own story. Beyond that, getting this question settled has been a major factor in fully restoring a positive attitude toward God. Sorting this issue out has solved a key intellectual problem, a problem that only heightened my own emotional and spiritual pain. What has happened and is still happening to Pat still hurts very deeply, but at least my frustration and anger over the situation are no longer directed toward God. Believe me, there is a very uneasy feeling that comes with being angry at the only person who can solve your problem. Thank God, that uneasy feeling and that anger are gone!

I have also shared this at length, hoping it will help my reader. Though no one's circumstances will be exactly identical to mine, we all need to be reminded how easy it is to build an incorrect case against God through inferential reasoning. Before looking at circumstances and inferring that God has deceived you or done anything else wrong, remember that the conclusion you are drawing may not be the only one possible. It is more likely that you are reading the evidence the wrong way. Before you accuse God over what you think he has done or failed to do, look again at the evidence, and be sure that you have interpreted it correctly. If you look long enough and hard enough, I am certain you will see that God is not guilty of any wrongdoing.

What about the other question that began this book? Could one seek, find, and do God's will and get affliction in response? If by this we are asking whether God would respond to our obedience by sending affliction as a punishment, the answer is an obvious no. God does not send suffering as a punishment for doing his will. The Bible amply underscores that the one who obeys God will only receive blessing from God's hand in response to that obedience. The God of the Scriptures is not an evil fiend who rewards us for obeying him by punishing us with pain and suffering.

On the other hand, there is more to the question than just this. While God will not punish with affliction for obeying his will, doing God's will does not guarantee that there will be no affliction when we obey. This sounds paradoxical, but it is not. God will not send affliction in *punishment* for our obedience, but if we are faithful to God's plan, Satan will not be pleased. The adversary often takes out his displeasure by afflicting the people of God. The truth is that the more we are in the center of God's will, the more we are capturing ground against the enemy of God. Hence, the more we obey God's will, the more we can expect Satan's attacks on us in an effort to discourage and dissuade us from accomplishing God's purposes.

Yes, there will be affliction when we do God's will, but it doesn't come as punishment from God's hand. Scripture is very clear that those who follow God are engaged in a war with those who don't (Eph. 6:12; 1 Peter 5:8-9). Satan will do his best to destroy us and our faith, but the book of Job should encourage us that there is nothing he can do that the Almighty does not know, permit, and control. We are engaged in a spiritual war. Do we think we can go to war, even in the front lines of the battle, and never be wounded?

I was. But I never expected a wound quite like the one we got. I have come to see, however, that this expectation was unrealistic. The enemy is very real and has many ways of attacking those who would follow the Lord. Knowing there will be battle wounds does not mean the wounds do not hurt, but it can help us assess more accurately what has happened. One may wish exemption from the battle, but that is not possible. One may even think of changing sides, as many do when confronted with tragedy; but that option is not the answer to our problems for either time or eternity.

I trust that what you have read will minister to your needs and help you serve others who are hurting. This has not been an easy book to write, and I would give anything not to have learned what I have through these experiences. But if this book helps you, then it will have been worth the effort to write it.

As for me and my family, the story isn't finished yet. Just as there have been surprises already (some welcome, some unwelcome), God probably has others in store. Do I have any regrets over marrying Pat and having a family? In many respects, that is an impossible question to answer. If it means would I have married her if I knew then what I know now, that doesn't make the question any easier. If I knew then what I know

now, I would have known what a blessing from God she and my sons would be. I would have known all the problems I'd avoid by not marrying her, but I'd also have known of the lost blessings. Would I give back those incredible blessings to escape the trials we have experienced? Who would be so foolish, even if they thought they could guarantee an easier set of trials or avoid troubles altogether?

I do know some things for a certainty, though. I know that throughout eternity I'll be thanking God for the wife and family he gave me and for the ministry he has allowed us to have in spite of (and even because of) the many hardships. I also know that when the wounds from the spiritual warfare in which we all are engaged come, and they will come, we will need the comfort and care of God. In spite of our reactions, even if we suspect or actually accuse him of wrongdoing, I am so thankful that he is still ready to give his comfort and care!

AFTERWORD

by Patricia S. Feinberg

I WOULD LIKE TO TELL YOU WHAT GOD HAS DONE IN MY LIFE. As my brother and I were growing up, our mother suffered with a mysterious disease. I did not know the name of the disease, nor the specifics of it, because we were not told. My personal opinion was that it was a mental illness, and most of my mother's symptoms suggested that to me. It was only much later that we would learn she had Huntington's Disease.

My family was not a Christian family at the outset, but the Lord gave both my mother and me a desire to know him. My mother sold Avon products for a while, and she made a friend on her route who was a Christian. My mother's friend invited her to an evangelism meeting where she accepted Christ. The pastor from the friend's church came over and talked with my father, who also became a Christian. My brother and I came to the Lord when a missionary candidate from the church came to talk with us.

I was nine years old at the time. As God gave me a desire to follow him, I started reading my Bible every day and attending the church. Over the years I became very involved in the church.

The youth pastor in the church had been a missionary to Africa, and he was a great influence on me. When he preached at a missionary conference where an invitation was given for young people to follow the Lord completely in their lives, I turned my life over to God for whatever he wanted me to do. I thought he might want me on the mission field, so I took steps to prepare myself for that. I went to Nyack College, in part because it had a strong reputation for training missionaries. After graduation, I applied to some mission boards, but nothing opened up. Therefore, I went on to Wheaton College for an M.A. degree in Christian education. I felt such additional training would help me in mission work, and I thought that after further academic work, the Lord would open up the opportunity for me to go to the mission field.

While at Wheaton, our prayer group prayed that if the Lord had a husband for us, he would bring him along at the right time. One of my friends in the group was dating a student at Trinity Seminary, and she arranged a "blind date" for me with another seminarian attending Trinity.

DECEIVED BY GOD?

A Journey Through Suffering

As it turned out, John and I dated not just once but many times. As our relationship grew, the Lord made it clear that he wanted us to marry. We felt certain that God had led us together. After several years of marriage, we were blessed with three special boys who have been a continual joy to us.

In the midst of raising a family and sharing in John's ministry, I learned in the fall of 1987 that I have a genetic neurological disease called Huntington's Chorea. It involves the premature deterioration of the brain, and it can have severe mental and physical effects. In addition, it shortens one's life. Though I was extremely shocked when this disease was diagnosed, I knew that when physical problems come, one should thank God for his presence and strength in the midst of those problems, rather than becoming bitter. And I knew that I should do that whether I felt like it or not; so that's what I did on the way home in the car. I also knew 1 Thessalonians 5:18 which says, "Give thanks in all circumstances, for this is God's will for you in Christ Jesus." No matter what the circumstances, God is still there, and he is in control of all that happens. He is faithful to his Word. That is reason for thanksgiving, and I continue to thank him each day.

The next months were very difficult for both John and me, going through the process of accepting what had happened. One thing that was very helpful to me was that as I read through the book of Psalms, I wrote down every reference having to do with God's strength in time of trouble. The main one was Psalm 46:1, "God is our refuge and strength, an ever-present help in trouble." God made that verse true in my life. I have confidence in his presence, even in the midst of this disease.

I have been trying to figure out what God wants me to learn from this, and what he wants me to do about it. One thing the Lord has reinforced to me is that I am just clay in his hands. As Paul says in Romans 9:20, "But who are you, O man, to talk back to God? Shall what is formed say to him who formed it, 'Why did you make me like this?'" God has the right to do anything he wants with me. Who am I to complain?

I gave myself to Christ as a teenager for whatever he wanted—without reservation. Though what has happened is not at all what I imagined, I cannot complain. I said he could do with me as he chose. Far from complaining, it is my responsibility to thank God for doing his will in my life.

Another thing God has done through this illness is to make me face life and death issues and to see the absolute necessity of making the most of the time I have left. It is easy for all of us to think there will be enough time to do what needs to be done for the Lord. We tend to plan to serve him, but always later. My experience is a vivid reminder that no one of us has a guarantee of how long our life on earth will be or what kind of life we will have. Whatever God calls us to do in service of the kingdom needs to be done sooner, not later.

Another Scripture that God has used in my life is 2 Corinthians 1:3-4—"Praise be to the God and Father of our Lord Jesus Christ, the Father of compassion and the God of all comfort, who comforts us in all our troubles, so that we can comfort those in any trouble with the comfort we ourselves have received from God." The Lord has given me such complete comfort that I want to find ways to share it with others.

My disease has also offered witnessing opportunities. One opportunity that John and I had was the chance to witness to my Jewish neurologist. John went with me to see her, and she came right out and asked us what he was doing teaching in a Christian seminary when he has a Jewish last name. In telling her how his family came out of Judaism to Christ, he was able to share the Gospel with her. The other thing that she could not understand was how calm we were about the whole thing.

I consider it another blessing of the Lord that the disease has for many years progressed extremely slowly. That has amazed the doctors from the beginning, and it gives us a further opportunity to witness to them. When they express their amazement, we make a point to share our belief that my disease and my very life are in God's hands. I believe the course the disease has taken is a result of God's intervention on my behalf.

JOHN S. FEINBERG

——— ∞ ———

Afterword by Patricia S. Feinberg

It has been many years since we learned that I have Huntington's. God has been so faithful to me, and I thank him for his faithfulness, love, and comfort. It is my hope that what I have shared will be a comfort and encouragement to you, the readers. I want to say to those who are suffering that God is sufficient!

NOTES

Chapter 1: Prelude to a Problem

1. Alvin Plantinga, *God, Freedom, and Evil* (New York: Harper & Row, 1974), pp. 63-64.

Chapter 7: Using Affliction for Our Good

1. See my *The Many Faces of Evil* (Grand Rapids, Mich.: Zondervan Publishing House, 1994), chaps. 1–12.

ABOUT THE AUTHOR

John S. Feinberg is Professor of Biblical and Systematic Theology at Trinity Evangelical Divinity School in Deerfield, Illinois. He has been a visiting professor of theology and ethics at various schools in Europe.

Feinberg has a B.A. degree from UCLA, an M.Div. degree from Talbot Theological Seminary, a Th.M. degree from Trinity Evangelical Divinity School, and M.A. and Ph.D. degrees from the University of Chicago.

He is the author of *The Many Faces of Evil*, *Theologies and Evil*, and *Ethics for a Brave New World* (with Paul D. Feinberg). He was editor of *Continuity and Discontinuity* and co-editor (with Paul D. Feinberg) of *Tradition and Testament*. He was one of four contributors to *Predestination and Free Will*. He has written numerous scholarly journal articles.

Feinberg and his wife, Patricia, live with their three sons in a northern suburb of Chicago.